T0327092

The Crusades Uncovered

PAST IMPERFECT

See further
www.arc-humanities.org/our-series/pi

The Crusades Uncovered

Adrian J. Boas

ARCHUMANITIES PRESS

British Library Cataloguing in Publication Data
A catalogue record for this book is available from the British Library

ISBN (print) 9781641894784
e-ISBN (PDF) 9781641894791
e-ISBN (EPUB) 9781641894807

www.arc-humanities.org
Printed and bound in the UK (by CPI Group [UK] Ltd), USA (by Bookmasters), and elsewhere using print-on-demand technology.

Contents

List of Illustrations vi

Preface vii

Chapter 1.   Perceptions 1

Chapter 2.   Places. 27

Chapter 3.   People 71

Postscript: Hit and Myth—History and Mystery 93

Further Reading 97

List of Illustrations

Figure 1. Jean Miélot's painting of Jerusalem,
           fifteenth century 7

Figure 2. Louis and Douglas Solomon (1915). 28

Figure 3. The Horns of Hattin. 31

Figure 4. Crac des Chevaliers. 35

Figure 5. Belvoir Castle. 37

Figure 8. Aerial photograph of Akko. 52

Figure 9. Pietro Vesconte's map of Acre,
           fourteenth century. 58

Figure 10. Mount Tabor. 63

Figure 11. Hospitaller rural estate centre, Aqua Bella.. . . . 67

Figure 12. Sultan's Pool (Germain's Pool), Jerusalem. 86

Preface

In memory of my friend in the field,
Ronnie Ellenblum (1952–2021)

I had never intended to become an archaeologist. Archaeology is not the first profession that comes to mind for a child growing up, as I did, in Australia. However, history has always captivated me, its seeds perhaps planted on long ago Saturday afternoons when, with no other occupation, I would leaf through three huge scrapbooks that a great-great-uncle had put together in the 1880s. They transported me back to a different world, to a time that was somewhat obscure, yet somehow familiar, a sepia past of horse carriages, gas lamps, dark interiors with overly elaborate furnishings, bearded gentlemen in frock coats and top hats, women in black lace dresses with high collars, elaborate head gear, silk flowers, ribbons, and black jet jewellery, and children who might easily have stepped out of a Tenniel illustration from *Alice through the Looking Glass*. If the present sometimes seemed dull, the past appeared to be full of interest. And it may be that a curiosity about the Middle Ages began to evolve back then as well. A favourite children's book was *Nicholas and the Wool-Pack* by the English author, Cynthia Harnett, a tale about rural life in late medieval England. And I wonder if a fascination in medieval knights might have had its source in a famed national hero, an armour-bearing bushranger who, in his final showdown with the police, dressed himself and his gang members in medieval-looking suits of armour fashioned from plough mould boards. But certainly none of this would have led me down the path I have taken, were it not for the move my family made when I was sixteen, all the way across the world to a place where the past mingled with the present, a land of Biblical scenery, studded with walled cities, battlefields, and fortresses, where one could pick up an Iron Age stone tool in a field, speak and be understood in an ancient language, shop in a medieval bazaar, carry in one's pocket coins impressed with the same designs found on coins minted two millennia back. As I discovered the rich history of the Holy Land, I became acquainted with the crusades; through field trips to castles and battlefields and through a great deal of reading, that led eventually to academic studies and the decision to make a career of exploring, studying, and teaching about the crusades and about Frankish settlement in the Levant.

Over the years I have worked on surveys and excavations of many different sites—cities, villages, and fortresses—but most of my career has been devoted to the exploration of the ruins of one of the greatest crusader fortresses—Montfort Castle in the western Galilee, the chief fortification of the German Teutonic Order in the Holy Land. The excavations at Montfort are in a way indicative of the changes that archaeology has undergone over the past century. Montfort was the very first crusader castle to be excavated. In 1926 a small team sent out on behalf of the Metropolitan Museum of Art in New York in search of a thirteenth-century suit of armour, uncovered a large part of the upper ward of the castle. That venture, although it resulted in a thoughtful study of the castle and its material remains, started out with the limited aim of finding a specific object to fill a gap in a museum collection. It was not untypical of the period. By the time of our renewed project at Montfort eight decades later, archaeology was no longer a form of "treasure-hunting," but a serious scientific field of study.

The title of this volume was suggested to me by my editor in order to distinguish these short studies as the works of an archaeologist. I was initially inclined to choose something else, perhaps because I have never felt entirely comfortable with the limitations of this professional label, and also because these particular writings, originally published as bi-weekly blog posts, are not only about archaeology, and indeed, not only about the crusades. They are about science and art and architecture; they are about travel and nature, memory, and nostalgia; they are about the present, the recent past, and the more distant past. But in retrospect, the suggested title is probably the most appropriate one, for the crusader period is the thread that I have chosen to bind all of these issues together, and indeed I have spent a considerable part of my life uncovering the crusades, or to be more precise, uncovering evidence of the Frankish presence and settlement in the crusader states.

Archaeology entails much physical effort, with pick and hoe, heaving buckets and barrows, sweeping, dusting, brushing. It involves long hours in the summer heat, and it requires rising in the early mornings, working through the long days, and finally trudging up steep hills and over rocky terrain at the end of the day for an all too brief respite before getting back to the work of sorting, recording, and writing up. Archaeology is an earthy activity. The archaeologist breathes the dust, smells, and tastes the soil. He lives in nature, his companions are not only fellow archaeologists, students, and volunteers, but snakes, scorpions, and fleas, hawks flying above, wild boars rummaging through the undergrowth, and jackals howling across the valley at dusk. This closeness to nature is a good thing, not only for the opportunity it provides to observe it at close range. It breaks down barriers with the past and brings one closer to the experiences of the people one is investigating. What better way to understand a labourer who was once engaged in building a fortress, or a soldier who lived in and battled over it, than to dig into its foundations, and in doing so, to inhale the same dust and perspire under the same harsh sun? At the end of a morning's work at Montfort, hoeing the earth, clearing sage bushes, gingerly lifting rocks and taking care that there are no venomous creatures lurking beneath, you acquire an intimacy with the labourer who eight centuries ago on this very spot, cautiously upturned these stones, hoed into this same earth, uprooted these same fragrant plants. Add to that the profound emotion one experiences when holding in one's hands an object that some unknown and long-forgotten individual had held ages ago. This is indeed a remarkable vocation and this closeness with the past is a large part of its appeal. The "outdoorness," the being-in-nature aspect of fieldwork, has a particular appeal for academics who might otherwise spend their entire lives at their desks, the only dust they breath being that which has settled on library shelves. And there are other appealing aspects. Archaeology is detective work. The past is a puzzle, a plot—partly seen, mostly obscured. It needs to be slowly and painstakingly exposed, analysed, put back together. The archaeologist is a Sherlock Holmes or Hercule Poirot, who must apply his intuition, his "little grey cells" in order to make heads or tails of what he has found.

After having physically exposed the past, the archaeologist has another task, an additional "uncovering" to carry out, albeit an abstract one—the interpretation of what has been found in academic papers, lectures, and books. The following digressions represent one form of this second, cerebral "uncovering," in this case mini-essays, informative but casual, drawing on my earlier blog posts. Archaeology exposes chronologically – from the present to the past. In the sections below I have taken a less restricted approach, moving from the past to the present and from the present to the past and back again, and through partly autobiographical accounts and musings, I have tried to show how archaeologists and historians can respond to such a complex and contested subject as the crusades. I have grouped my reflections under the categories of Perceptions, including subjects such as travel, legends, warfare, and wonderment; Places, under which I consider the battlefield of Hattin, Crac des Chevaliers and other fortresses, Jerusalem, Acre, Mount Tabor and the countryside of the Holy Land; and People, where I discuss Guy de Lusignan, Marino Sanudo, Germain, and Saladin; before making some closing remarks on how history reverberates in time. Mine is a personal approach. Each historian's story is unique, but a personal approach is, I believe, the best way to bring the past to life, and I hope through these ponderings to entice a new generation to engage in this field.

Chapter 1

Perceptions

Dream delivers us to dream,
and there is no end to illusion.

Ralph Waldo Emerson, "Experience"

Travel[1]

Aldous Huxley referred to travel as a vice, "...imperious, demanding its victim's time, money, energy and the sacrifice of comfort."[2] That is true enough, but like all vices it also provides a gratification that makes the adversity seem somehow worth putting up with, at least in retrospect.

The "delights" of modern air travel are considerable: the sleepless night before, the rush to get to the airport in time, the fear that one has forgotten something (passport, e-ticket, toothbrush), the endless zigzagging queues, the need to half-undress at the security counter with a line of people waiting on you (removing the belt from your trousers becoming a herculean task). And then there is the cramped seating space, the unpalatable airline food, screaming chil-

---

[1] This section was written prior to the current COVID-19 pandemic, which has made the unpleasantries of the following few lines seem such trivial discomforts.

[2] Aldous Huxley, *Along the Road. Notes and Essays of a Tourist*, 2nd ed. (London: Chatto, 1948), 11.

dren in the seat in front and the seat behind, the sleep-forsaken night, and finally more endless zigzagging queues, the need to half-undress yet again, and the long wait for one's suitcases that are invariably the last to appear. And in the back of our minds, the thought is hovering ominously; in a fortnight or so we will have to go through the whole process once again. Enough to discourage any would-be traveller you might think. And yet thousands board planes every day, brace themselves, and go through these experiences with varying degrees of patience, acceptance, and annoyance.

It might ease our doubts about whether it is worthwhile making the effort, if we compare present-day travel to the experiences of the medieval traveller going by ship to the Holy Land. Instead of several hours, their trip took several weeks each way, and they travelled under conditions that we would regard not only as intolerably uncomfortable, but categorically provoking fate. Instead of the occasional frightful moments of turbulence that we occasionally experience, travellers by ship not infrequently encountered terrifying storms that would last for hours or days. In size, medieval ships were closer to modern river ferries than today's ocean liners, and the monstrous superliners, those floating hotels that even today stun us for their enormity, could not have been imagined. But the small vessels were crowded, with up to a thousand travellers, passengers, and crew. And on these long journeys, the average medieval traveller had no more legroom than does his or her modern airline counterpart—a space about the size of a grave (an uncomfortable and occasionally appropriate comparison). And rather than a padded seat in an air-conditioned cabin, these berths were flee-ridden mattress on the floors of dark and stuffy holds. Food was poor, water was sometimes scarce and often hardly palatable, there were rats (rarely encountered on airlines), and there was livestock (ditto). The latter was brought on board to be consumed during the journey, or to provide milk or eggs. Theft was rife, seasickness and various illnesses were commonplace. The proximity of neighbours, generally strangers, left the traveller exposed to abundant discomforts. Many of one's companions could, no doubt, have done with a good bath (though, one suspects, the medieval sense of smell may have been somewhat blunted). At night one had to put up with loud snoring and the commotion of those who did not wish to sleep. And there was the difficulty of making one's way in the dark to relieve oneself when the need arose, as it frequently must have, particularly as dysentery was almost universal.

I have often tried to get my head around the idea of what it must have been like for those mostly inexperienced and unsophisticated travellers who set off across the sea on a pilgrimage or a crusade. They faced much more than discomfort. Boarding small wooden ships, they must have felt rather like astronauts feel on taking the elevator up to a tiny space capsule atop a metal container filled with a couple of million litres of highly combustible rocket fuel that is about to be set alight. And like those astronauts, as the ship set off, they must have asked themselves, what in heaven's name had possessed them to take such a risk? This analogy with a spaceship comes naturally for someone like myself who grew up through the 1950s and early 60s. I was in kindergarten when the Sputnik burst onto the pages of newspapers and flickered onto television screens, not ours, as at that time my father still regarded television as an object of depravity (one he would later succumb to). I remember each new space-related event from that first satellite to the flight of the dog Laika, and the names of each astronaut or cosmonaut, from Gagarin to Titov and Shepard to Glenn. I even managed, when I was nine, to persuade my mother to permit me to get a crewcut, a hair style that had become a popular homage to the heroic Mercury astronauts (and one that I today sport, though no longer by choice). I was fascinated by the idea that people could actually be up there on a tiny white light that looked no different from the other countless stars except that you could see it moving its own path slowly across the deep and silent ocean of eternal darkness.

Fearful it must have been, but full of fascination as well. And through the accounts of their travels, we get a glimpse of this medieval outer space. Pilgrimage accounts open a window into many aspects of the Holy Land under Frankish rule that we might otherwise have missed—its strangeness, its sanctity, and its allure, but also its severity, brutality, and desolation. And in the best of these accounts, we get to know the traveller, and we gain a sense of his excitement, fear, restlessness, wonder, and spirit of adventure.

Rorgo Fretellus (fl. 1119–1154) was a pilgrim from the County of Ponthieu in northern France who went to the Holy Land around the year 1110, and subsequently remained in the East, eventually becoming chancellor for the Prince of Galilee and later still, archdeacon of the patriarchate of Antioch, or possibly of Nazareth. In the preface to the 1896 translation of Rorgo's pilgrimage account, *Liber locorum sanctorum terrae Jerusalem*, James Rose Macpherson wrote critically about the manner in which the description hops about from one place to another without any sense of organization: "…one finds it impossible to say much in praise of its orderly arrangement," although he admits: "…in this respect our unknown author is not unlike many of the other pilgrim writers."[3] But I think that it is precisely this mercurial quality that makes Rorgo's and other similar accounts so much more vivid and human, and gives us, their readers, a real sense of a medieval pilgrimage and what it involved.

Rorgo (his artlessness seems to demand first name intimacy) begins his description in the city of Jerusalem, but quite abruptly he turns south to Bethlehem, then heads back to the neighbourhood of Jerusalem. Next, he is off to the Jordan River near Jericho, then down to the Dead Sea, back up to Hebron, and down to the Dead Sea again. Then he rambles on for a while about the route of the Exodus, before returning to his own itinerary, where he is now heading north to Damascus, then south yet again, this time to the sources of the Jordan, the Sea of Galilee, Nazareth, Mount Tabor, Samaria, Nab-

---

3 Rorgo Fretellus, *Liber locorum sanctorum terrae Jerusalem*, trans. James Rose Macpherson, Library of the Palestine Pilgrims' Text Society 5, no. 1 (London: Palestine Pilgrims' Text Society, 1896).

lus, once more to Jerusalem, to Bethlehem, and then back to Jerusalem. He doesn't seem to stop to catch his breath! And if you are not yet giddy with all this fitful darting about, he turns north once more, and then south to the neighbourhood of Hebron, back down to Jericho, northwest to Lydda and along the coast to Caesarea, Acre, Tyre, Sidon, Beirut, and Tripoli. And he could hardly end without making a final return visit to Jerusalem. He seems rather like a nectar-intoxicated insect, fluttering abruptly about in a field of spring flowers. And in a way, for the medieval pilgrim, the possibility of visiting all these wonderful holy sites must have been not unlike that of a bee encountering the explosion of colour and smell in an April meadow.

To what extent Rorgo's vertiginous tour represented his actual movements is impossible to say. It could simply be that this description is the product of his erratic mind at some later time going over and over recollections of what he had seen. We do not know precisely when or where Rorgo's account was written, but quite often, it seems, these accounts were composed long after a pilgrimage had ended. Alternatively, like so many other pilgrims, he may have made Jerusalem his base, from there heading out for day trips or longer. That would explain the sporadic quality of this text. And not all the *itineraria* are quite so mercurial. Some pilgrims arrived at a certain port, usually Jaffa or Acre, and set out from there on a logical and systematic route. But there are others accounts that are not so different from Rorgo's. They vary in style, length, and detail, and some are almost telegraphic and give little information beyond a list of places visited and routes taken. But the best of them are remarkably informative, describing not only the roads and the holy loci, but things of everyday nature, relating to daily life in the places visited; markets, houses, people, and natural surroundings—things that make these texts a source of great value for the historian and indeed for any interested reader.

One such source is a text composed by a Dominican friar, Burchard of Mount Syon. He gives us a picture of the kingdom of Jerusalem in the years just prior to its fall in 1291, and it is one of the most detailed and informative accounts of the Holy Land that survives from the late the thirteenth century. He describes its borders, its flora, fauna, and its inhabitants. Of Burchard himself, who probably originated in Magdeburg in northern Germany, we know little, but his text is very well known, having been repeatedly copied and, in later times, printed. There are over one hundred surviving manuscripts and around twenty printed editions prior to 1746, some of them accompanied by illuminations, maps, diagrams, and city plans. There are long and short versions, modern editions including the best-known critical edition by Johann Laurent published in 1864, translations into German and French and later into English, and a recently discovered extended version from the British Library.[4]

In 1455 the Duke of Burgundy, Philip the Good, had his secretary, the scribe, translator, and gifted illuminator Jean Miélot, prepare an illustrated translation of Burchard's text. Of the illuminations in this edition, best known is Miélot's full-page rendering of the Holy City of Jerusalem.

In it he created a city of towers and domes, blending fact and fantasy, with an obvious preference for the latter. There is some realism, albeit vastly exaggerated, in his depictions of the Church of the Holy Sepulchre and the buildings on the Temple Mount, but the rest is entirely fiction, a fantasy of blue and gold. The crescent of Islam is above the *Templum Domini*, as indeed it would have been when Burchard

---

4 See *Peregrinatores medii aevi quattuor*, ed. J. C. M. Laurent (Leipzig: Hinrichs, 1864), 3–94. Pringle, *Pilgrimage to Jerusalem and the Holy Land*, 241–320. See also John R. Bartlett, "Burchard's *Descriptio Terrae Sanctae*: The Early Revision," *Palestine Exploration Fund* 145 (2013): 61–71. For a detailed account of all the editions and much else see Ingrid Baumgärtner, "Burchard of Mount Sion and the Holy Land," *Peregrinations. Journal of Medieval Art and Architecture* 4, no. 1 (2013): 5–41. The newly discovered version was published by Jonathan Rubin, "Burchard of Mount Sion's *Descriptio Terrae Sanctae*: A Newly Discovered Extended Version," *Crusades* 13 (2014): 173–90.

Figure 1. Jean Miélot's painting of Jerusalem, fifteenth century.
Bibliothèque nationale de France, Paris.

was there, but the city is a wholly oriental one, with nothing but the Holy Sepulchre to show its recent Christian past, although that past would still have been manifestly evident. It is very different from the twelfth-century maps of Jerusalem, the only detailed contemporary representations of the city under Christian rule, which, for all their symbolism present a reasonably faithful layout of the crusader city. By the fifteenth century Jerusalem had, in the minds of Westerners, moved away from reality and had become a mystical city of the imagination.

Legend

A picture book that I particularly enjoyed as a child was called *Hit and Myth*. It was one of those books with large illustrations of different animals on each page, and with the pages cut width-ways across the centre, and the illustrations so carefully placed that if you kept the top of the page open on one animal, and flicked through the lower halves, each turn would display another weird hybrid creature. It was amusing to me then because, even for a child at an age when so much that is encountered is discovery, certain things were understood. Farmyard animals could be relied upon to play by the rules—a cow was a cow, and a horse was a horse. The idea that there might be an animal that was half horse, and half rooster was nonsensical, and consequently delightful. I had not yet encountered such absurdities as the three-headed frog of Weston-super-Mare in England, or Stumpy, the four-legged Hampshire duck. As one grows older the world is found to be an ever less predictable place.

Because there is indeed absurdity in the world, people are occasionally willing to believe in the existence of extremely bizarre things, and often fall victim to hoaxes. The north American Jackalope, a sort of antlered hare (hence its name, which combines jackrabbit and antelope), was a taxidermy hoax of the 1930s that gained much popularity at the time and survives even today as a modern myth. It was described as an aggressive creature and one that had the ability to imitate the human voice. Another rather delightful deception originated about the same time in a café in New York where, in order to drum up business, the owner took a goldfish bowl, filled it with water, and placed on it a sign informing the public that it contained invisible fish from South America. The prank was so effective that the police had to be called in to control the crowds. Susceptible to the existence of strange things is certainly enhanced when they cannot actually be seen. When they can, even if they are real, they sometimes provoke a great degree of scepticism. When a pelt and sketch of an Australian platypus was first observed in London in 1798, the scientists, not surprisingly, regarded it as a forgery. One wonders what they might have thought about the far more strange, horned, and hairy, tentacled creatures with huge jaws, vast teeth, and hundreds of eyes that we are able to observe today through the lens of an electron microscope.

A year before those practical scientific minds of Great Britain dismissed an actual creature as a hoax, Friedrich Schiller wrote a poem, *Der Kampf mit dem Drachen*, in which he described the infamous dragon of Malpasso, a creature that was perhaps no more a hoax than was the platypus:

> Why run so fast the hurtling crowd
> Down the long streets, roaring loud?
> Is Rhodes on fire?—more fast the strong,
> Wedg'd close and closer, storms along.
> High o'er the train, he seems to lead,
> Behold a knight on warlike Steed!
> Behind is dragged a wondrous load;
> Beneath what monster groans the road?
> With wide jaws like the Crocodile,
> In shape a Dragon to the sight,
> All eyes in wonder gaze the while—
> Now on the Monster, now on the Knight.

Schiller's poem tells the story of a certain Dieudonné de Gozon, a knight of Languedoc, who, according to the popular myth, had succeeded where others failed in killing a famous dragon that had become a serious threat to the locals and their cattle in the valley below Mount St. Stephen, south of the city of Rhodes. Gozon was in fact a historical figure. He became a local hero, and his popularity eventually led to his appointment as the 26th Grand Master of the Hospitaller Order in 1346. The dragon too appears to have existed, and its head was on display on one of the city gates of Rhodes until 1837, when it was removed during repair work. Schiller's comparison of the jaws of the dragon of Malpasso to those of a crocodile, may have been closer to the mark than he imagined, for the dragon may simply have been a huge crocodile that had originated in the Nile. This might sound far-fetched, but Nile crocodiles (*Crocodylus niloticus*), like other saltwater crocodiles, are known to be capable of swimming in the sea for considerable distances. Into the early twentieth century crocodiles were to be found in the Crocodile River near Caesarea, some 380 kilometres distant from the Nile where they had originated, proof that they could indeed cover considerable distances. A huge crocodile found in a place where such creatures were not normally known, and the tendency of people to exaggerate when describing unusual things that they encounter, might well have led to the birth of the myth recorded by Schiller.

In the right circumstances it is easy enough to believe in unlikely things. In Rome, back in 1977, I saw a screening of Stephen Spielberg's UFO movie, *Close Encounters of the Third Kind*. Leaving the cinema with friends at the end of the movie, as we walked out into the narrow, crowded streets of Trastevere I noticed that people were pointing up to the sky. Looking up I saw something bright, large, oval, and flashing, that was moving very slowly across the bit of dark sky visible between the buildings. I imagine that I was no different from most of the people who had just left the cinema in being, for just a few moments, convinced that I was witnessing the appearance of an unidentified flying object. In fact, it was, nothing more sinister than the Goodyear blimp. Susceptibility to visions is even more prevalent when people find themselves in extreme circumstances, such as in battle. Nor is it unusual for people who hear about visions by someone who is convincing, not only to believe that this person has indeed witnessed what he describes but, in some cases, to come to believe that they themselves have witnessed it. During the First Crusade, when, after a prolonged siege the crusader army occupied the city of Antioch, the Christians in turn found themselves besieged by a vast Muslim army under the leadership of Kherboga, the governor of Mosul. Fear and fatalism descended on the crusader camp, but with the miraculous discovery, in one of the city churches, of what was claimed to be the Holy Lance (the lance that pierced Jesus on the cross) the crusaders regained their conviction that God was on their side. With renewed courage they attacked the besieging enemy, and then something even more remarkable occurred. Here is a description of the event in the near contemporary *Gesta Francorum*:

> There came out from the mountains, also, countless armies with white horses, whose standards were all white. And so, when our leaders saw this army, they were entirely ignorant as to what it was, and who they were, until they recognised the aid of Christ, whose leaders were St. George, Mercurius and Demetrius. This is to be believed, for many of our men saw it.

Joined by this heavenly host the Christian victory was assured. And this was not the only example of heavenly assistance during the crusade. Raymond of Aguilers described a vision experienced the following year at the siege of Jerusalem:

> On this day, the Ides of July, Lord Adhemar, Bishop of Puy [who had died earlier, at Antioch], was seen in the city by many people. Many also testified that he was the first to scale the wall, and that he summoned the knights and people to follow him.[5]

---

5 The *Gesta Francorum* and Raymond of Aguilers quoted from *The First Crusade: The Chronicle of Fulcher of Chartres and Other Source Materials*, ed. Edward Peters (Philadelphia: University of Pennsylvania Press, 1998), 223 and 260.

We might be tempted to dismiss these stories as examples of the credulity of a more gullible age. But UFO sightings aside, there are examples of more recent occurrences of a similar nature to those described above. On April 30, 1915, a London-based Roman Catholic newspaper called *The Universe* carried a story under the headline "On A White Horse: St. George and Phantom Army." It described an event that it claimed had occurred in August 1914, during the opening phase of the First World War. At the time, the British Expeditionary Force was desperately trying to stave off the German advance through Belgium. A letter, said to have been written by a British officer from the front, described how, as he led a company of about thirty men in a desperate attempt to break out from their surrounded trench, he became aware that they were being joined by a phantom army, a large company of men with bows and arrows, led by an officer riding on a great white horse.

The story was not original, nor was it trustworthy. It was in fact a rather transparent lifting of a fictional account titled "The Bowmen" that had been published the previous year in the *London Evening News*. That account had been written by Arthur Machen, a Welshman best known as an author of supernatural, fantasy, and horror fiction. Despite its imaginary origins, following the publication of this story in *The Universe*, numerous "eyewitness" accounts appeared supporting this supposed vision. These apparitions and the widespread support they received, certainly seem to suggest that there is a case for amending the saying "Seeing is believing" to "Believing is seeing."

* * *

But not all crusader legends are about unlikely creatures or ghostly apparitions. Many are about actual crusaders, heroes, anti-heroes, and tragic characters. Take the case of Jaufre Rudel, a troubadour from Aquitaine who died during the Second Crusade (1147–1149). Here is a crusader whose principal motivation for going on crusade was not to fight the infidel and free the Holy Sepulchre, but rather a somewhat pathetic obsession he had developed for a married woman whom he had never actually seen. The story of Rudel, inspired perhaps by his own poetry, records how he joined the crusade after hearing returning crusaders speak of the great beauty of the Countess Hodierna, wife of Count Raymond II of Tripoli. According to this legend, she became his *amor de lonh*—his distant love. Sadly, for him, however, on his way East he fell ill, and when he finally disembarked at Tripoli he was already dying. The countess herself came down to see him, and, not to miss such an ideal opportunity, Rudel promptly died in her arms.

Probably the only truth to this story is that Rudel did in fact die in the East. Nonetheless, the tale circulated, and later inspired a host of nineteenth-century Romanticists. Among these were the poets Johann Ludwig Uhland, Heinrich Heine, Robert Browning, Edmond Rostand, and in particular, Algernon Charles Swinburne who recorded the story in several works including *The Triumph of Time* and *The Death of Rudel*:

> Her gold hair, heavy and sweet,
> Clothes her straight from face to feet,
> As she stoops the tresses meet.
> Ah, dear Lord, I prayed for it,
> I have had her kiss.

Well, some consolation at least. But my undoubted favourite use of this tale is in the delightful dialogue between Bertie Wooster and the highly sentimental Madeleine Bassett in P. G. Wodehouse's *The Code of the Woosters*:

"Oh, Bertie [said Madeleine Bassett], you remind me of Rudel."

The name was new to me.

"Rudel?"

"The Seigneur Geoffrey Rudel, Prince of Blay-en-Saintogne."

I shook my head.

"Never met him."

"He lived in the Middle Ages. He was a great poet. And he fell in love with the wife of the Lord of Tripoli."

I stirred uneasily. I hoped she was going to keep it clean.

"For years he loved her, and at last he could resist no longer. He took ship to Tripoli, and his servants carried him ashore."

"Not feeling so good?" I said groping. "Rough crossing?"

"He was dying. Of love."

"Oh, ah."[6]

Warfare

I went to sea in September 1952 aboard the RMS Orion, sailing from Perth to London, and then on the RMS Queen Elizabeth from Southampton to New York. By the time my parents, my brother, and I reached New York, about an eight-week voyage, I had spent more than half of my life at sea, and I think that this places me in the position to be regarded as something of an authority on sea-related matters.

We tend to think of crusader battles as having generally taken place on dry land, and this is by-and-large true, although there was active participation of the Italian fleets in transporting crusaders East, in the sieges of the coastal towns during the first decades of the twelfth century, in the siege of Constantinople in 1204 and in sieges of Damietta on the Nile in 1218–1219 and 1249. But naval victories are less likely to come to mind when we contemplate the crusades, and not everyone is aware that ships played a decisive role in the 1099 conquest of Jerusalem. In a manner of speaking, the crusader conquest of Jerusalem might be regarded as a naval victory, even though, like another famous battle, the Battle of Midway during the Second World War, it did not involve engagement between ships of opposing fleets. At Midway, the two fleets never actually saw each other, and not a single shot was fired by ships on either side at the enemy. In the siege of Jerusalem, only one of the engaging sides employed

---

6 Quotation courtesy of the P. G. Wodehouse Estate, Rogers, Coleridge & White Lit. Agency.

ships, and the battle took place on dry land nearly sixty kilometres from the Mediterranean shore.

The Battle of Midway on June 4–6, 1942 is regarded as a decisive victory for the United States, one that put an end to Japanese dreams of additional territorial conquest in the Pacific. Although a large number of vessels were involved on either side, including three American aircraft carriers, and four aircraft carriers of the Japanese fleet, the battle took place when the two fleets were a considerable distance from one another, and all the fighting took place in the air. Within no time at all American pilots had sunk three of Japan's carriers, and by the end of the engagement the Japanese had lost their four carriers and a heavy cruiser, along with 3,500 men and 270 aircraft. American losses consisted of one carrier, one hundred men and a hundred and thirty aircraft. This American victory prevented Japan from taking the strategic island of Midway, and effectively ended its role as an important naval power.

The siege of Jerusalem has not surprisingly entirely eluded the notice of historians of sea warfare. It was played out in the summer of 1099, and was an engagement between the army of the First Crusade and that of the Fatimids of Egypt who held the Holy City at that time. Prior to the arrival of the Christians, the Egyptians had cut down all the forests and disposed of the timber in the vicinity of Jerusalem, leaving the crusaders, who apparently did not bring any siege weapons with them, with no material with which to build ladders, towers, and siege machines. Without these, they were incapable of overcoming the city's defences: its walls, forewalls, and moats. This difficulty delayed the conquest for several weeks but was finally resolved when some Genoese galleys that were anchored in the port of Jaffa were dismantled and their timber was brought up to the Holy City where they were reconstructed as three large siege towers. Two of these towers were destroyed in the ensuing battle, but one was brought up against the northern city wall and the troops climbing it entered the city, opened the gates, and brought about the conquest of Jerusalem and two centuries of Latin rule in the Holy Land.

One wonders if, when scaling the siege tower on the morning of July 15, Litold and Gilbert of Tournai, the two Flemish brothers who were the first to go up, had any awareness of the fact that they were climbing up what had formerly been perhaps masts, deck-boards, or part of the prow of a galley, and that they were therefore participating what was arguably the greatest naval victory of the Middle Ages.

* * *

One of the most potent modern images of failure, as powerful perhaps as that of the Air America helicopter evacuating American citizens on a rooftop in Saigon in April 1975, was a photograph of the shell of burnt-out U.S. navy Sikorsky helicopter in the Iranian desert in April 1980, following the failed attempt to release Americans taken hostage by the fundamentalist Iranian regime. (Helicopters so often produce poignant images of failure; one recalls another burn-out helicopter in which were the bodies of Israeli Olympic athlete hostages, victims of a failed rescue mission by German police snipers at Munich airport in September 1972 and the recent abandoned Chinook helicopters at Kabul airport left by the Americans withdrawing from Afghanistan in the summer of 2021.) Of the eight helicopters that took part in Operation Eagle Claw, only five managed to arrive in working condition at Desert One, the first staging area of the operation, and after the decision was made to abort, one of them crashed into a Hercules transport plane. The failure of the mission not only cost the lives of eight members of the task force aboard the destroyed aircraft, but effectively ended the presidency of Jimmy Carter, and left the fifty-two members of the embassy staff to face an additional eight months before they were finally released from captivity.

As with any other period, crusader history is composed of successes and failures. There are many events to demonstrate this, and the First and Second Crusades are as good candidates as any, perhaps even the best. Whereas the First Crusade was a resounding success that enabled the establishment of a kingdom and the commencement of two centuries of Christian rule in the Holy Land, the Second Crusade was a complete disaster, a farcical, misguided affair that achieved nothing positive whatsoever. There is no dramatic image of this failure, but failure it was.

If Eagle Claw was perhaps primarily a case of bad luck, the failure of the Second Crusade was the outcome of mismanagement with a little treachery thrown in. The crusade came as a response to the first great territorial loss of the crusader period—the conquest by Imad ad-Din Zengi, atabeg of Mosul, of the County of Edessa in 1144. Two years after it fell, the city of Edessa was briefly recovered by Joscelin II, but he failed to take the citadel and Zengi's successor, Nur al-Din retook the city later the same year. The crusader response was somewhat remarkable. Instead of a concerted effort to recover Edessa, or to take Aleppo, the seat of power of the Zengid dynasty, the crusade was detoured to Damascus. This change in plan was decided upon on June 24, 1148 at a council held at Palmaria, south of Acre. All the contingents had arrived in the Holy Land, and, among those participating in the council were many royals, bishops, dukes, barons, and others. The participants included the German Emperor Conrad, King Louis VII of France, King Baldwin II of Jerusalem, and the masters of the military orders. Baldwin and the Templars appear to have been the driving force behind the Damascus detour, and it is probable that with the dwindling size of the crusading army, neither Conrad nor Louis had any great desire to take on such substantial targets as Aleppo or Edessa. Both were more distant and possessed more formidable defences than those of Damascus. We remain in the dark as to the precise motivation behind the council's decision, but if Aleppo or Edessa were not to be the focus, the southern Syrian city was not an entirely unlikely choice, for, although it had actually allied with the Franks, as William of Tyre notes, it remained "a city of great menace to us."[7]

---

7 William of Tyre, *Chronicon*, ed. R. B. C. Huygens, Corpus Christianorum, Continuatio Mediaeualis 63A (Turnhout: Brepols, 1986), bk. 17, chap. 2; in English as *A History of Deeds Done Beyond the*

On May 25 the united Christian army moved east to Tiberias, from there north to Banias and then to Daria on the outskirts of the Syrian city. Baldwin and his army were in the lead, the French under Louis in the middle, and Conrad and the army of the Germans at the rear. The plan was to first take the surrounding countryside with its orchards and fields. This strategy was decided upon because Damascus was dependent on its surrounding lands for food and water. The blockade was expected to weaken the city to the point that it would fall into their hands like ripe fruit. However, the dense orchards were well-defended by towers, and the Christians found it extremely difficult to advance along the narrow paths that traversed them. William of Tyre suggests that the attack was directed on the north. If so, having approached from the south the army must have skirted the city. Ibn al-Qalanisi, the Damascene chronicler, wrote that the Franks arrived first at Manazil al-'Asakir to the south and from there moved southeast to al-Mizza.[8] Presumably, from there they continued skirting the city on its eastern side to the north. Conrad and his troops managed to gain control over the Barada River which flows from northwest, and this indeed gave the Franks control over the food and water of the region. Everything at this point was going as planned, and it appeared that victory was assured. But then the crusaders made a disastrous decision. They quite suddenly decided to move back down to the southern side of the city. William of Tyre suggests that this move was promoted by some disloyal Franks who were "led on by avarice" and were in league with the Damascenes.[9] They persuaded the king and other leaders to make this move, pointing out than on the southern side of the city there were no orchards and the approach to the walls would be easier. It proved to be a fatal error, for what it

---

Sea, trans. Emily A. Babcock and A. C. Krey, 2 vols. (New York: Columbia University Press, 1943), 2:186.

8 Ibn Al-Qalanisi, *The Damascus Chronicle of the Crusades*, trans. H. A. R. Gibb (London: Luzac, 1932; repr. Mineola: Dover, 2002), 283.

9 William of Tyre, *Deeds*, ed. Babcock and Krey, 2:191.

in fact meant was that the crusaders now found themselves without the food and water that they had had in abundance in the north. As they had expected a short campaign, they had brought few supplies with them. Once they made this move, they were unable to return north as the Muslims were quick to regain control of the orchards and to strengthen their defences. There may have been other factors at work. Al-Qalanisi suggests that the Franks had received word of the approach of vast Muslim reinforcements.[10] In any case the whole thing was a fiasco. Once they realized that they could not rectify it, they ended the siege and returned home.

Who were the traitors responsible for this disaster, and what had they received from the Muslims for their treachery? Sadly, William of Tyre gives us no clue, but many assume that they were Templars, and that they had received substantial bribes. Whatever the truth, this great international effort, the first crusade to be led by European royalty, went down in history as a dismal failure. It put a damper on the idea of the infallibility of a crusade, and it strengthened the Zengids, easing the way for Nur al-Din to expand his control over Syria and ultimately to take Damascus in 1154. For the Christians, the only substantial achievement of the Second Crusade had nothing to do with the Latin East and took place before the armies had even arrived in the Holy Land. A contingent from the British Isles that had been forced ashore near Porto due to bad weather, joined the forces of King Alfonso I of Portugal in attacking Moor-held Lisbon, and recovering it. The only other European effort of the crusade was a series of attacks carried out by Saxons and Danes against the pagan Welds in the Baltic region, but that ended in nothing more than insubstantial truces.

The Second Crusade was not the first failure of the crusading movement. That distinction perhaps goes to the Crusade of 1101, the so-called Crusade of the Faint-Hearted, the only achievement of which was the recovery of Tartus (Tortosa), or to an even better candidate, the Peasants' Crusade of 1096,

10 Ibn Al-Qalanisi, *The Damascus Chronicle*, trans. Gibb, 286.

which achieved nothing whatsoever. Nor was it by any means the only one to lose direction. The crusades of Louis IX also have that distinction. But failure it certainly was, and without a consolation, such as that of another famed detour—the Fourth Crusade, which at least established a brief-lived empire and achieved major territorial gains for the Venetians.

Wonderment

I recently saw a video report in which a ten-year-old boy who had been colour blind since birth was enabled, with the aid of special glasses, to see colour for the first time. The expression on his face was spellbinding. He was undergoing an entirely new experience, simply by being able to observe what had been there all along. Most of us have the capacity to see, but we are so used to what we see that we are rarely able to really appreciate it. Aldous Huxley described examining simple things around him after taking the drug mescaline, and this appears to have been a very similar experience to that of the colour-blind boy. He too was seeing things that he had frequently seen in the past in a very different way. "This is how one ought to see..." he wrote, "...how things really are."[11]

I have never taken hallucinogenic drugs, partly because the opportunity never arose, partly because I am a fairly responsible person, but mostly, if I am to be perfectly honest, because I am not very brave. I mark it down in my list of missed life experiences, for better or worse, like skydiving or mountain climbing. But I am capable, on occasion, of observing things as if for the first time, simply by deciding to do so. Indeed, this is something that can be experienced by anyone, without the use of drugs or special glasses. It is simply a matter of decision. We can choose to experience anything around us, with any of our senses, more acutely. Put a raisin on your tongue, a single raisin, and slowly suck the sweetness out of it. There is no taste more intense. Observe a flower you have

---

11 Aldous Huxley, *"The Doors of Perception" and "Heaven and Hell"* (1994; London: Vintage, 2004), 19.

looked at countless times in the past. But this time really look. Notice how robust, how pure the colour is, how it radiates, how it contrasts so sharply with the objects around it. As we age, we lose our awareness of possessing this ability, but it is always there. I recall my eldest son as a new-born baby, his arm raised above his head, observing his tiny hand for the first time, inches from his face, his eyes and mouth open in incredulity. That sort of experience decreases as the world and all its strangeness becomes more and more familiar to us. But look at your hand, now. Is it not truly remarkable? We need to recover the ability to be amazed, to experience enchantment in the world around us.

Today we occasionally find wonder in new technologies, new discoveries. But in the past, wonderment was a state that was easier to achieve. People led much more restricted lives, rarely leaving the places in which they were born, rarely encountering people of other cultures, or indeed anything out of the ordinary. The exceptions were merchants who occasionally travelled great distances, people who went on crusade or pilgrimage, and those who left Europe in the wake of a crusade to settle in the East. But merchants, crusaders, and settlers rarely left written accounts of what they experienced. So, we turn to the pilgrims, particularly churchmen who were among the few people in medieval society who were literate, and capable of recording what they observed. In their writings we get a sense of the amazement they felt on encountering strange and fabulous things. It is often so profound that, in documenting it, rather like children they sometimes allowing themselves to slip into a space between real and imagined, with a penchant for the latter. And so, we read about a cave near Bethlehem where the Virgin's milk dripped from the walls, an image of the Virgin that when it was moved caused the rain to fall, a river that observed the day of rest by ceasing its flow, or alternatively, one that flowed only on the Sabbath, and another river that was so considerate towards the Christian faithful that it would supply multitudes of fish from three days before Palm Sunday to three days after. We hear of a strange sea "always smoking and dark, like the furnace of hell"[12] in the waters of which one could still observe ancient cities destroyed in a Biblical cataclysm, and which, on the anniversary of their destruction, still discharged stones, wood, and other remains. We discover a burial place outside the walls of Jerusalem, a pit in which the disposed bodies of the dead decomposed within just three days without giving off any foul smells. We read of a strange fruit called Adam's Apple on which the marks of Adam's teeth could plainly be seen, and an oblong fruit that grew on the trees of Paradise, a hundred touching one another on one bough, and tasting like honey (a banana, of course). And this sense of the miraculous is there even when the descriptions are entirely realistic. The chronicler John of Joinville, attending the French king Louis IX during his crusade, describes quite accurately a fossil shown to the king that had probably come from the Late Cretaceous limestone of Sahel Alma north of Beirut, or Hajula (Hjoula) or Hakel northeast of Jubail (*Giblet*):

> During the king's stay at Saida someone brought him a stone that split into flakes. It was the most marvellous in the world, for when you lifted one of the flakes you found the form of a sea-fish between the two pieces of stone. This fish was entirely of stone, but there was nothing lacking in its shape, eyes, bones, or colour to make it seem otherwise than if it had been alive.[13]

* * *

The popular 1970s bestseller by Peter Tompkins and Christopher Bird, *The Secret Life of Plants*, put the case for seeing plant life in an entirely different way from how it had until then been viewed. Plants, the authors claimed, have a profound consciousness or awareness. The difficulty for most of us in accepting this lies in the fact that it is well-nigh impossible to get a word out of them. The best we can hope for is a

---

12 Burchard of Mount Sion, in Pringle, *Pilgrimage to Jerusalem and the Holy Land*, 283.

13 Joinville and Villehardouin, *Chronicles of the Crusades*, trans. M. R. B. Shaw (Harmondsworth: Penguin, 1963), 315.

silent display of joyful emotion in the form of a new bloom, or melancholy in the form of withering leaves. And even when that occurs, can we be certain that it is not something that would have happened anyway, and has nothing to do with emotions. But the idea raised in this book that plants have much more in common with us, is perhaps not entirely new. It appears to get support from at least one medieval writer, perhaps two.

When visiting the region of Antioch in the thirteenth century, the German traveller, Wilbrand of Oldenburg observed a strange wild plant called *lesupubeledemis* or "Balsam of Jesus" which proved to have a remarkable high-strung character:

> On Good Friday people sow its pips, which grow up among the springing vegetation and at first produce white flowers, which afterwards change colour to green, then red, and finally yellow. These are then transformed into apples; and if anyone is disparaging about the beauty of them, saying that they [have seen] finer, the apple in question becomes angry, swells up and bursts apart into tiny pieces in indignation.[14]

Now, there you have a fruit with attitude. And in case his readers might think that he is being naïve in repeating such a seemingly outlandish tale, Wilbrand adds:

> And this is remarkable, seeing that the apple is non-rational; but we testify to what we have seen, and our testimony is true.

What Wilbrand is describing appears to be *Momordica balsamina*, a tendril-bearing annual vine, indigenous to tropical Africa and Asia, Arabia, India, and Australia. I recall seeing it growing on the fences of orchards in the coastal plain outside the town of Rehovot (where sadly the citrus trees have long since been replaced by apartment buildings). It produces round, lumpy, orange fruits, which when they are ripe, indeed burst open quite suddenly to reveal a rather nasty and toxic-looking interior of sticky, scarlet-coloured seeds.

---

14 Wilbrand of Oldenburg in Pringle, *Pilgrimage to Jerusalem and the Holy Land*, 73.

Another remarkable "apple" was described by our old friend, Rorgo Fretellus. He recorded a fruit known as the Apple of Sodom (*Poma Sodomitica*) that grows in the vicinity of the Dead Sea. While it does not display the highly-strung comportment of the *Iesupubeledemis* it is certainly remarkable in its deceptiveness and in its stubborn unwillingness to let go of the long-passed disaster that it witnessed and that was recorded in the Book of Genesis:

> In the lake are islands producing bright green apples, which appear most desirable for eating, but such that if one plucks them, they immediately shrivel up and are reduced to ashes, exhaling a smoke as if they were still burning.[15]

A pilgrim known simply as Anonymous V added:

> Round about the lake are trees which bear exceeding beauteous fruit; but the fruit stinks, and when you have plucked it, of a sudden, falls into ashes.[16]

These descriptions recall and are no doubt repetitions of those made by the first-century historian, Josephus Flavius (*Bellum Judaicum*, bk. 4, chap. 8, §4) and his near contemporary, Tacitus (*Historiae*, bk. 5, chap. 6). Josephus identified the ashes as those of the destroyed cities of Sodom and Gomorrah. Later writers also referred to these fruits. The Swedish traveller and naturalist, Frederik Hasselquist wrote in 1766 (*Voyages and Travels in the Levant, in the Years 1749, 50, 51, 52*) that the *Poma Sodomitica*, which he also referred to as "mad apples" (*mala insana*), were sometimes filled with dust. He gives a more scientific reason for this phenomenon, though one that is not at all correct, stating that they had been attacked by an insect that left only the beautiful skin intact. In truth, they are not apples at all, but the fruit of

---

15 Fretellus, *Liber locorum sanctorum*, trans. Macpherson, 13.

16 Anonymous V, in *Anonymous Pilgrims, I–VIII: 11th and 12th Centuries*, trans. Aubrey Stewart, Library of the Palestine Pilgrims' Text Society 6, no. 1 (London: Palestine Pilgrims' Text Society, 1894), 34.

the *Calotropis procera/Asclepias gigantea vel procera*, a small tree with cork-like bark. The fruit of this plant appears solid, but is in fact full of air, and when pressed it bursts in a puff leaving a few shreds and fibres from a small slender pod in the centre—the only useful part of the fruit, though not for consumption, but for the fine silk-like fibre that was used to make wicks. Other than the "ash" or "dust," their flesh contains a bitter sap that turns gluey on exposure, is hard to remove from the hands and is highly toxic.

The mysterious and hauntingly desolate landscape around the Dead Sea where these strange fruits grow is a setting designed to play on the imagination. It has a decidedly underworld quality that puts me in mind of another place I once knew. When I was about ten years old, perhaps a little older, my father would on occasion wake my brothers and sister and me in the middle of the night and take us off in his car on a nocturnal escapade. Our destination was the petroleum refinery at Altona on Port Philip Bay. He was a civil engineer with an expertise in matters of corrosion and he had some business or other to do there. He took us along for the company no doubt, but, as far as we were concerned, for the adventure. I never paid much attention to what he was doing—something relating to electrodes, anodes, and cathodes I seem to recall, which meant no more to me then than it does now. I found far more appeal in the car ride through the dark cool night, observing the monstrous landscape around us, the chimneys, pipes, smoke, and flames, enjoying the pleasure (as in those days it was) of passive cigarette smoking, and delighting in my father's good humour, his songs and his very, very old jokes. Soon, as we approached our destination, the smell of cigarettes was suppressed by the acrid but no less appealing smell of petroleum. There was excitement in the flickering lights of the refinery, in the tangle of silver and black pipes running alongside the road and rising up in skeletal constructions, and in the billowing plume of orange flame high above us that was burning off excess gases. Here was the delightfully named Cat Cracker (nothing to do with the cracking of cats, but a construction used in converting raw petroleum into usable products), which, when it was built a decade earlier had been the tallest building in Melbourne and had become a well-known local landmark. There was a tremendous excitement in these night-time excursions to a place that would have made an apt setting for Dante's inferno.

A few years ago, I flew over the Dead Sea on the last lap of a return flight from Australia. It is today a third smaller in size than it was when I first saw it a little over five decades ago, and if it is not yet entirely dead, it is certainly dying. It is sad to see, as one clearly can from the window of a plane, how steadily it is shrinking. It appears to be heading towards the same fate as the Aral Sea in Central Asia. Nonetheless, it remains a paradoxical place, one of desolation and of subtle and uncomfortable beauty. On the one hand it is hostile, shimmering under intense heat, a poisonous landscape with its gases, sink holes, salt encrustations. On the other, it is a place of remarkable beauty. The water is like glass, a smooth, pale grey-blue mirror, and in the progressively changing light of the day the hills surrounding it take on a variety of muted pastel shades, their solidity dissolving in the iridescent haze. It is indeed so bizarre and remarkable that one hardly wonders at Rorgo having believed that he could see in its clear water the ruins of ancient buildings, the remains of Sodom and Gomorrah.

Chapter 2

Places

I like places in which things have happened—
even if they're sad things.

Henry James, The Portrait of a Lady

Hattin

Among the photographs of family members that I have on
my desk is one of two half-brothers of my paternal grand-
mother. Their names were Louis and Douglas Solomon. The
photograph was taken in October 1915 in the Strand Studio,
London.

At the time, the brothers were in England recuperating
from injuries sustained in the Gallipoli debacle. In the photograph the two boys appear young, fresh-faced, but pensive
and somewhat subdued; rather different, I would imagine,
from how they might have appeared in a photograph taken a
year earlier, before they had experienced the horrors of war.
Louis served in the 2nd Field Ambulance and was wounded
on August 22, 1915. He may have participated in the Battle
of Hill 60 that had been launched the day before. It was the
last major assault of the Gallipoli Campaign. On the day he
was wounded, the attack had been reinforced by the Australian 18th Battalion, which consisted of newly arrived troops
that were inexperienced and ill-equipped. Attacking at dawn
and using only bayonets, they suffered 383 casualties. After
his recuperation Louis remained in service. He subsequently

Figure 2. Louis and Douglas Solomon (1915).

served in France where he was injured again on March 23, 1918. Douglas was a reinforcement in the 10th Battalion. He is recorded as having fallen ill, probably with dysentery or typhoid fever, both of which were rife among members of the battalion, and on July 13, 1915 he suffered a back injury. But his early discharge in 1916, at which time he is recorded as suffering from "shell-shock and loss of power of limbs," is rather more telling. Shellshock was a new "disease" in 1915, increasingly recognized but hardly understood. The term first appears in February that same year in an article by Charles Myers the consulting psychiatrist of the British Expeditionary Force published in *The Lancet*. Soldiers suffering from it were often returned to the battlefield, and on occasion were put on trial and even executed, for cowardice or desertion. The horrific physical outcome of this misunderstood malady, suggested by the words "loss of power of limbs" can be observed in films of inflicted soldiers taken at the time.[1]

Being nearer to us in time and so much more extensively and realistically recorded, the horrors of the two world wars and of other recent conflicts seem far more appalling than those battles of the remote past. Manuscript illuminations of knights in battle do not quite get across to us the sense of horror of those battles, even when, as is often the case, they are illustrated graphically and show hacked-off limbs and heads sliced with axes and swords. As works of art, such illuminations can be beautiful, colourful, and detailed. Take, for example, those of the famous thirteenth-century Morgan Bible in which biblical scenes are rendered in medieval dress. They are detailed and skilfully illustrated, but as records of warfare, something is missing. There is no emotion, hence, despite their occasionally explicit subject matter, they still appear as beautiful objects that cause us no revulsion. Here is a man on horseback—a sword has sliced right through his helmet and a spear has pierced his body. Blood is gushing

---

[1] For example, the short film *War Neuroses*, which shows severe cases filmed at Netley Hospital in 1917 and Seale Hayne Military Hospital (both in the UK) in 1918.

from the wounds, but he remains static, impervious, even, in some cases, smiling, as if nothing at all had happened, rather like the dismembered Black Knight in Monty Python—"Tis but a scratch...." These illustrations arouse none of the horror, disgust, and depthless pity that we feel on observing photographs of rotting bodies in the muddy trenches of northern France and Belgium. This, I suppose, is the difference between photographs and other forms of artistic expression, for, because of its stark realism, a photograph, even a bad one, can achieve a degree of emotional intensity that can rarely be attained in other mediums, and then only by the greatest of artists. For all the ability of an artist to influence the composition and create dramatic effects, what the photographers saw is what we see.

I don't think that I ever encountered these two ancestors of mine, although they might still have been around when I was a child. But looking at the photograph, I feel that I do know them. I can see them just as did the man behind the camera. His eyes have become mine, and these two boys, Louis and Douglas, seem almost to be here, or perhaps I am there with them in the studio. And I can see in their faces something of what they have been through. In his *Camera lucida*, Roland Barthes gives many examples of this triangular relationship, this rapport between the observer of a photograph, the photographer, and the photographed.

But if medieval illuminations fail to bring us close to the event as photographs can do, words are sometimes able to cross the barriers of time. Just as the poems of Wilfred Owen, Isaac Rosenberg, and Edmund Blunden can take us into the horror and pity of the Great War trenches, and can wrench our hearts as effectively as any cold and cruel photograph, so the Muslim historian, Imad ad-Din through his brutal language is able to take us onto the slopes of Hattin just after the battle was over and give us a real sense, if not the personal anguish, of the horror of a medieval battle:

> The dead were scattered over the mountains and valleys, lying immobile on their sides. Hittīn shrugged off their carcasses, and the perfume of victory was thick with the stench

Figure 3. The Horns of Hattin.

of them. I passed by them and saw the limbs of the fallen cast naked on the field of battle, scattered in pieces over the site of the encounter, lacerated and disjointed, with heads cracked open, throats split, spines broken, necks shattered, feet in pieces, noses mutilated, extremities torn off, members dismembered, parts shredded, eyes gouged out, stomachs disembowelled, hair covered with blood, the praecordium slashed, fingers sliced off, the thorax shattered, the ribs broken, the joints dislocated, the chests smashed, throats slit, bodies cut in half, arms pulverized, lips shrivelled, foreheads pierced, forelocks dyed scarlet, breasts covered with blood, ribs pierced, elbows disjointed, bones broken, tunics torn off, faces lifeless, wounds gaping, skin flayed, fragments chopped off, hair lopped back skinless, bodies dismembered, teeth knocked out, blood spilt, life's last breath exhaled, necks lolling, joints slackened, pupils liquefied, heads hanging, livers crushed, ribs staved in, heads shattered, breasts flayed, spirits flown, their very ghosts crushed; like stones among stones, a lesson to the wise.[2]

---

2 *Arab Historians of the Crusades Selected and Translated from the Arabic Sources by Francesco Gabrieli*, trans. from the Italian original

This evocation is so powerful that it echoes even today when I drive up the narrow dirt road towards the saddle-shaped hill of Hattin, dust billowing across the fields and the heat building up around me in a blinding haze.

All about, the land drops away—gently but steadily to the south, more severely to the north, and east where the lake shimmers beyond the cleft of Arbel. The sky too is shimmering, and the lake is white. I stumble breathlessly up the long-dormant volcanic crater that dips like an empty bowl. A path cuts across the dry grass, and the crater is bordered by a few stumpy trees and piles of boulders that were once fortifications of a town, forgotten long before the Frankish knights and foot soldiers sought refuge here from the failing battle. In this silent place it is the setting that evokes the battle. Of physical remains there is almost nothing to connect it to the events of that morning in 1187 and to the battle that changed history. The one exception seems to be an abject relic—a low pile of scattered stones among the thorns at the highest point of the southern horn. It formed the base of a small structure that some believe to have been erected by one of the participants in the battle. It looks like nothing at all, but the excavator proposes that it is the remains of a monument constructed by Saladin himself to commemorate his great victory over the Christians. And indeed, there are records of such a monument, a Dome of Victory mentioned in thirteenth-century Muslim and Frankish sources.[3] Perhaps indeed that is what it was, but it is now so unimposing that one cannot but harbour doubts.

There is a second memorial at Hattin. This one did not set out to commemorate the medieval history of this site, yet it is perhaps in some ways allied to it and it is certainly no less remarkable than Saladin's alleged monument. It stands at the foot of the crater—an odd, squat obelisk of highly pol-

---

(1957) by E. J. Costello (London: Routledge and Kegan Paul, 1969), 135.

3 Zvi Gal, "Saladin's Dome of Victory at the Horns of Hattin," in *The Horns of Hattin*, ed. Benjamin Z. Kedar (Jerusalem: Yad Izhak Ben-Zvi / Israel Exploration Society, 1992), 213–15.

ished black granite. It was placed here in 2014 by an American Pentecostal church, the Church of God, a denomination that believes that this hill was the site of the Sermon of the Mount. It replaced an earlier monument and was, so the church representative says, placed here as an act of love. On one side of the monument is inscribed the Biblical precept: "Thou shalt love thy neighbour as thyself." But its erection appears to have had the opposite effect, and in certain quarters it has been regarded as a provocation, an act of antagonism. And so, somebody has gone to a great effort to scratch away all the inscriptions on its sides, quotations from the Psalms, the Book of Isaiah, and the Gospel of Mark. In the end it has become a monument to intolerance, and as such it is perhaps a more fitting memorial for the site of a great battle between two religions.

Monuments aside, you cannot go to Hattin and come away feeling indifferent. It is like a vast stage setting. Perhaps you need to know something of the play in order to really appreciate it, but the ambience of this place is so powerful that it must impress even upon the entirely uninitiated viewer an awareness that this was the scene of a great drama. The hill itself is not remarkably high. Yet it is seen from afar from all around, and it has an unfathomable quality that does not relate to size. It rises, or rather hangs over the landscape just as Vesuvius does…dark, foreboding, dominating, uncompromising, filling the silent void with a visual rumbling of its volcanic origins. The further one leaves its proximity and moves out into the landscape, the greater one's awareness of its lurking presence, a black sentinel watching over everything from above, like an eagle scanning the fields for the tiniest of movements. And when one goes away, it remains, an image cast on the retina of memory like a brilliant light that lingers when the eyes are closed.

Hattin had a long history before 1187, perhaps an important one. There is here the as yet unexplored Late Bronze and Iron Age city, the walls of which crown the crater like a black wreath. It may have been the Biblical Adamah (Joshua 19:36) a Hebrew name which means "soil" or "earth" (אדמה), and the name Hattin possibly comes from the Hebrew Hitim (חיטים), meaning "wheat." Both are appropriate appellations for this place of rich volcanic soil. But that distant past beneath the rubble of its walls remains unnoticed, forgotten, eclipsed by the more recent drama. The fact that even the battle that gave the place a name in human memory has left almost nothing to be observed today (an archaeological survey carried out in the vicinity has only produced a few negligible fragments of iron), is not remarkable. Its historical impact makes it easy to forget that this was after all, a fleeting event, taking place on a single morning, and all over in just a few hours. In this regard, battlefields are often a disappointment. We see empty landscapes. We do not see the troops; we do not hear the noise or smell the gunpowder. We see nothing of the heat of events, nor even of the pitiful scene on the morrow, such as Imad ad-Din saw at Hattin. Old battlefields do not live up to the expectations that their names evoke in our minds. And this low black hill casts a penumbra over that dramatic day in July 1187. So, we are left to speculate—what if the king had not fallen into Saladin's trap? What if he had not been so rash as to leave the safety of the Springs at Saforie. What if he had by-passed the hill and headed on to Tiberias? If things had not panned out as they did, we might see King Guy as the great Christian hero. Everything would have been different. There would have been no Third Crusade, Jerusalem would have remained Christian, Cyprus might not have become a crusader kingdom, and Saladin would have been regarded as an impetuous bumbler, and just another forgettable figure in the pages of history. But this is how it is. Single, spur-of-the-moment decisions change the course of events, and reputations are made and lost by chance as much as by acumen or imprudence. But this volcanic mound...it surely would have found its notoriety whatever the circumstances.

Fortresses

If battlefields conjure up a sense of drama, a moment of time, a transitory event, fortresses remind us of the long-term real-

Figure 4. Crac des Chevaliers.

ity, and in an ironic way, by their very might they evoke a sense of insecurity.

In 1941 my father was serving in the Royal Australian Artillery in Syria. While on leave in Tripoli he ran into his admired older brother, a captain in the 2/23 Infantry battalion, who took him up into the hills to see the huge crusader castle of Crac des Chevaliers. I recall from my childhood seeing his tiny black and white images of the castle, some of which I still possess. My father never spoke much about this experience, except to recall that at the castle my uncle had got him intoxicated on the strong local beer, though apparently not to a degree that prevented him from taking the photographs. I have often wondered how much of an impact the great Hospitaller fortress made on him, but when he spoke about it, it was only to recall his delight at the reunion with his brother. Nonetheless, I imagine that it would have fascinated him, even in a somewhat inebriated state, as it must certainly for anyone who visits it. Monumental in size, remarkably intact, and with the finest medieval technology displayed in its defensive works, it is not hard to see why the Oxford undergraduate, T. E. Lawrence (later Lawrence of Arabia), referred to it in his 1910 thesis on crusader castles as "perhaps the best preserved and most wholly admirable castle in the world."

Crac is every castle-lover's dream. It is brilliantly perched, overlooking the Homs Gap—a green fissure that slices east across Syria from the coast. The gap was a natural feature that served as a perpetual threat to the unity of the mainland crusader states—the principality of Antioch and part of the county of Tripoli located to its north, and the rest of Tripoli and the kingdom of Jerusalem to its south. It was this geological anomaly indeed that necessitated the construction of Crac and other great military order castles to defend it. So, if the Franks were perhaps not pleased by the existence of the gap, we certainly can be. The physical features of the landscape and how they might be used by an enemy, frequently played as important a role in the development of the crusader fortresses, as did the size and actions of enemy armies. Crac was intelligently designed and incorporated all the innovations of this most innovative castle-building age. It was possibly the greatest achievement of military order architecture, and for medieval castles, we might almost say, it is what the Parthenon is for Greek temples.

The demographic weakness of Frankish settlement in the crusader states is well known. Apart from the few occasions when great crusading armies arrived on campaign from the West, the small population was a constant handicap in their conflict with the Muslim opponents, as it continued to be throughout the two centuries of Frankish rule. As they were incapable of changing this reality, the Franks applied their resourcefulness to introducing efficacious solutions. Predominant among these were two creations—the military order and the castle. The former was an entirely original innovation—an organization that was conceived as a means of providing soldiers with military training as part of a daily regimen, and of endowing them with the very best equipment available. The latter, the castle, was the most iconic of crusader creations. Castles were like limpets clinging to the rock in an inhospitable and stormy sea. Their role was complex and varied, but primarily their function was to remain standing. Castles were

Figure 5. Belvoir Castle.

defensive rather than offensive. And they were always strong. Through their strength they enabled even small garrisons to hold out for an extended period in the face of superior attacking forces. If they were strong enough, they would compel an invading Muslim army into a protracted siege, and that was the bane of any army that was formed of agricultural peasant warriors led by land-owning emirs, none of whom wished to be kept away from their fields for long periods of time.

In order to face the enemy and whatever military equipment he might possess, the castle had to be appropriately enhanced with defensive features and arrangements. In this regard, one of the best known of crusader castles, Belvoir, is an important lesson on the need to keep a finger on the pulse of an opponent's capabilities and advances in tactics and weaponry. When the land at Belvoir was purchased by the Hospitaller order in 1168 on a strategic site overlooking the Jordan Valley and the eastern frontier of the kingdom, the Hospitallers had in mind to construct a state-of-the-art castle. They chose an ancient design, one that had already been employed for several other crusader fortresses—the so-called *quadriburgium*—an enclosure castle with four projecting corner towers from which its garrison could defend the exterior walls from firing positions. To this design they added another long-established technique of concentric defensive lines, and at Belvoir this was done for the first time by enclosing one *quadriburgium* within another, thereby creating an almost symmetrical design and achieving a degree of perfection never before attained in any crusader castle.

Yet, having reached an apogee in castle design, the Franks promptly abandoned it, and with a single exception in a smaller fortress in western Cyprus, nowhere else in the Latin East did they return to the remarkable layout of Belvoir. The reason for this appears to be that at the very point in time when the Franks had achieved this pinnacle of design, it had lost its relevance, and it seems that it was the new siege weapons being employed by the Muslims that made this design redundant. The *quadriburgium* had been highly effective in its ability to limit the approach of an enemy by foot or on horseback, but the introduction of a powerful new ballistic weapon, the counterweight trebuchet, which appeared in the Latin East at about the time Belvoir was under construction, radically changed the playing field. Employing a massive counterweight, that was hoisted into the air and, when required, suddenly released, this new trebuchet proved to be a far more powerful weapon than any that had previously been used. A machine of this type, placed even some distance from the walls, would leave Belvoir and castles like it exposed in their entirety.

The design at Belvoir of a masterpiece of defensive symmetry shows the Franks at the peak of their abilities in fortification. Their immediate abandonment of this design shows them at the peak of their perspicacity. The introduction of the counterweight trebuchet had necessitated a fundamental rethinking. It was not enough to make the defences higher and more massive. Taller and thicker walls might slow down the attacker's efforts in breaking through, but they alone would not be enough as the trebuchets could fire over the top of them and cause a great deal of damage to the more vulnerable roofs and interiors. With the use of large machines even the thickest of walls would be vulnerable. The effective range of the trebuchet, depending on the position of the machine and the size and weight of the projectile, was around two hundred metres, so the most efficacious means of counteracting this new threat was to build beyond their range and on hills with slopes too steep to enable the attacker to bring them closer. A realization of this led to the construction in the late twelfth century, and through the thirteenth, of ever more complex and advanced fortifications, but more important, fortresses that took into consideration the lay of the land, the one thing that could effectively neutralize the effects of the trebuchet. They began, almost exclusively, to build the great spur and hilltop castles that became ubiquitous in the thirteenth century. These were invariably creations of the military orders, for it was the military orders alone that had the financial means to construct them. They had the inevitable flaws and weak points, but a combination of strength (walls were in some cases over thirty metres in height and up to ten metres thick), good design, and locations out of range of the trebuchets, made them more impregnable than any of the earlier fortresses.

There were always a number of factors at play in deciding upon the location for building a castle, and sometimes, some of these factors were of such significance that they outweighed the lessons learnt through experience. When this was the case, there would occasionally be a price to pay. Almost every visitor I take to Montfort Castle asks the same question—why was it built in what appears to be an entirely inappropriate location? It is situated on a hill that is considerably lower than the hills surrounding it, and to reach it one descends when approaching from the east. This would have put it at a distinct disadvantage when an enemy was advancing from higher ground, and it also meant that the castle would have had little strategic value, as its prospect over the surrounding countryside was limited to the area of the two converging valleys to the north and south. Most castles, even quite small ones were built overlooking vast areas and, as a consequence, they could also be seen from great distances. It was clear to everyone living in the shadow of a well-placed fortress who the overlord was. The question of why the German order chose this untypical and apparently disadvantageous location to build their principal fortress has long been debated. The only answer that seems to carry any weight is that their aim was the direct opposite of the standard rule—to make the castle less visible, and as far as possible, to hide it from their rivals, the two great military orders, the Templars and Hospitallers. For the Germans, these older, wealthier, and more powerful orders were, if not as formidable adversaries as the Muslims, certainly a challenge to their continued independence.

Of course, a vast stone fortress is impossible to hide. But placing it lower than the surrounding hills meant that only upon approaching fairly close to it could the castle be observed. Everyone knew it was there, but they could not see it. It was a matter of "out of sight, out of mind." The castle, hidden behind the hills, was not constantly calling attention to itself, as it would have been, had it been observable from a distance. In this manner the Germans hoped to avoid having it become a red rag for their rivals.

* * *

Castles were not built for beauty. In an essay titled "Architecture and Social Questions," Bertrand Russell wrote that, in the medieval world, beauty was to be found in churches and building of commerce, whereas "...castles were designed for military strength, and if they had beauty, it was by accident."[4] This is true to the extent that in building their fortresses, as opposed to churches, the architects did not set out with beauty chiefly in mind. Even the greatest fortresses have comparatively little architectural decoration to show, and what they have is usually limited to ceremonial halls and chapels. Most architectural decoration in Crac is found in the porch of the knight's hall, in the hall itself where there are

---

4 Bertrand Russell, *In Praise of Idleness and Other Essays*, new ed. (1935; London: Routledge, 2004), 29.

some fine sculptural pieces, and in the chapel where there are frescoes. Elsewhere decoration is limited and subdued. In Château Pèlerin ('Atlit), decorative sculpture can at present only be seen in the hall of the north tower and in most other castles decoration is reserved mainly for chapels and great halls. Montfort is something of an exception in the quantity of its decorative elements, chiefly architectural sculpture along with wall-painting and stained-glass windows that appear to have decorated all the domestic as well as ceremonial parts of the castle.

Rather than beauty, castle-builders sought strength, and a visual display of strength had a practical defensive purpose in that, seen from a distance it might deter an enemy from attacking. Nonetheless, castles were often beautiful in their overall appearance. If achieving beauty was not what motivated castles design, good practical design often goes hand in hand with beauty (as in nature which is always practical and often beautiful). If we consider beauty as an aspect of objects that makes them pleasurable to perceive, then there is a strong case for regarding many castles as beautiful, even if that achievement was not the object of the builder.

Jerusalem

When I was thirteen, I was given a set of phylacteries with silver cases. They were decorated on each side with images of four Holy Land sites beaten in the silver. One of these sites was Rachel's Tomb near Bethlehem, and of two of the others I have no recollection whatsoever. The fourth, however, I remember distinctly. It was the Tower of David. In reality it was what in modern times has appropriated the title that had once belonged to an entirely other edifice nearby. What it in fact displayed was a seventeenth-century minaret that had been constructed at the southwest corner of the fortress commonly referred to as the Jerusalem Citadel. A little irony here, for this sacred Muslim structure from which believers were called to prayer had become famous in its acquired identity on items of Judaica, while the "real" Tower of David, a building that incorporated the most substantial remnant of the three towers built by King Herod the Great of Judea in the first century BC, has been sidestepped (I almost wrote that it has faded into oblivion, but such a monumental mass of stone can hardly fade) and supplanted as a cultic decorative element with the much less remarkable, but more conspicuous mosque tower.

The association of both of these Towers of David with the famed Biblical king is of course entirely invented and both of them post-dated him, one by close to a millennium, the other by nearly two and a half. Despite some revisionist theories, the city of Jerusalem in the time of the Biblical king almost certainly did not extend as far west as Mount Zion. Indeed, King Herod had given the north-eastern tower of his fortress a different name—either Hippicus or Phasael (a matter of dispute among scholars), the former being the name of a Herodian general and close friend of the king, the latter, that of his older brother. The link with King David appears to have originated later; either in Byzantine times (fourth to seventh century AD) or subsequently, during the period of Muslim rule, when the tower became known as Miḥrāb Dāwūd—David's Prayer Niche. By the eleventh century, when Jerusalem was under Fatimid rule, the David connection was given a rather unexpected boost, when a famed rival of that earlier Jewish king was also commemorated in the city's defences. During a major program of refortification, a large, new tower was built in the northwest corner of the city, just inside the city wall, and was named for King David's best-known adversary—Burj Jālūt or Qasr Jālūt—Goliath's Tower. In the twelfth century, the Tower of David, now known in the Latin form—*Turris David*—evolved into something much more significant and formidable than a mere element of fortification. It became a symbol of lay rule, one that was placed alongside, and dominated symbols of ecclesiastical authority, just as, in the kingdom of Jerusalem, a lay regime dominated religious leadership. This new prestige finds expression on the royal seal, on which the tower appears in a central position, overshadowing the two most important religious structures of the Holy City that

Figure 6. The Royal Seal of Jerusalem.

appear on either side of it—the Church of the Holy Sepulchre and the former Dome of the Rock then known as the *Templum Domini.*

In this manner it very effectively demonstrates the tension that existed between lay and church authority, particularly in the early years of the kingdom, and it makes unmistakably apparent the lay perception of authority, with the state respecting, but dominating the church.

The tower's role as a manifestation of state authority can be observed in several pivotal events in which it served to establish the identity of the ruler of the kingdom. Whoever held the Tower of David ruled the kingdom. The first of these events occurred when Jerusalem fell to the army of the First Crusade on July 15, 1099. One of the principal leaders of the crusade, Raymond of Toulouse, whose contingent had been stationed nearby on the southern part of Mount Zion, reached the tower first, and promptly took hold of it, thereby de facto establishing himself as governor of the city, and potential ruler of the kingdom that was about to come into being. He was, however, quickly dispossessed of it when, after the city had fallen, Godfrey of Bouillon was elected as ruler. Initially Raymond tried to hold onto the citadel, claiming, according to William of Tyre, that he wished to retain it only until the Easter passage when he would return to Europe.[5] Godfrey, however, probably sensing that this was a ploy aimed at challenging his position of leadership, pressed for its immediate

---

5 William of Tyre, *Chronicon*, ed. Huygens, bk. 9, chap. 3.

surrender. When Raymond's own men, many of whom wished to return home, supported Godfrey's demands, the count had no choice but to give way, though he still held onto some vague hope, and rather than hand it directly over to Godfrey he gave it to the bishop of Albara, Peter of Narbonne, until the final decision would be made. But, in a bit of backhanded political scheming, the bishop promptly handed it to Godfrey, thereby putting an end to Raymond's manoeuvring. Already these events showed possession of the tower to be the supreme symbol of authority.

It was not long before the Tower of David played the same role for a second time. This came in the wake of Godfrey's death on July 18 the following year. The duke had promised to the patriarch that on his death both Jerusalem and its port, the coastal town of Jaffa, would be handed over to the Church. But this commitment appears to have been opposed by others in leadership, who set about attempting to forestall the handover and to make certain of the continuance of lay rule over the kingdom and the Holy City. For them it was imperative that possession of the tower be kept out of reach of the powerful patriarch of Jerusalem, Daimbert of Pisa, and of his supporters. A group of men faithful to Godfrey and intent on seeing his younger brother Baldwin of Boulogne inherit the kingship, prevented the patriarch from taking possession of the tower until Baldwin was able to reach the city from Edessa in the distant north.

A third time that possession of the citadel proved to be prerequisite to rule of the kingdom was in 1152. At that time, Baldwin III was attempting to put an end to the joint rule he shared with his mother Melisende, a condition that his minority had imposed upon him. Melisende refused to hand over the reins of power and took refuge in the Tower of David. It was vital for Baldwin to remove her from this symbol of rule, and in order to do so he went so far as to bring siege machines into the city and precede to bombard the citadel. Melisende was forced to concede to his demands and withdraw to Nablus, and so, for a third time, possession of the citadel proved to be the precondition for establishing rule.

The role of the Tower of David as "kingmaker" probably lay behind the decision, perhaps during the reign of King Amaury (1163–1174), to build the new royal palace adjacent to the citadel. This new palace is only known today by fragmentary remains exposed in archaeological excavations, but we may be able to get some idea of its appearance from an illustration of it that appears on the twelfth-century Cambrai Map of Jerusalem, where it is labelled as the *Curia Regis*. Here it appears as a two-storied structure surrounded by a crenelated wall, with towers either end and a porticoed and gabled solarium. It might be a fairly realistic illustration, and alternatively perhaps, pure invention, as indeed are the renditions of some of the other buildings on this map. It is impossible to say as so little of it has been found, but unlike that palace that has so completely disappeared, we can still observe the strength and grandeur of the Tower or David. It remains a potent image, even if its title has since been handed over to the much less remarkable nearby minaret.

* * *

A building that made a great impression on me as a child was the war memorial known as the Shrine of Remembrance, colloquially referred to simply as "the Shrine." It dominates Saint Kilda Road, a broad, leafy thoroughfare that leads from the southeastern suburbs of Melbourne into the city. As a public structure it was intended to commemorate an emotionally charged event; to pay tribute to the Australian troops whose lives had been lost in what was once known as the Great War. The First World War was a seminal event in the history of Australia. It is regarded as having been a major influence in forging a nation out of a colony. The Shrine is not a beautiful building. It is, however, vast, dominant, and austere. But perhaps what makes it most memorable is its strange eclecticism. Its architectural inspiration lay in two very different historical monuments; the Parthenon in Athens and the Tomb of Mausolus at Halicarnassus. The combination of these two influences on its design was viewed by many at the time as bizarre, and it came to be the object of much derision. Opponents referred to it as "too severe, stiff and heavy" and noted that "there is no grace or beauty about it" and it was scathingly called a "tomb of gloom."[6] It certainly is neither graceful nor beautiful, though the fact that it is gloomy might be regarded as the appropriate look for a war memorial. But architectural controversy generally fades. People become accustomed to buildings and their absurdities, and even the most despised architectural creations, when they survive long enough, come to be accepted, even loved, and regarded as representative of the places in which they are located. Think of the Eiffel Tower, which was considered by many Parisians when it rose over the city in 1887–1889 as useless, monstrous, "...something even those uncouth Americans wouldn't embrace" as some critics put it at the time. Julian Green, the Parisian born writer, himself the son of American parents, wrote that he many times wished it at the bottom of the ocean.[7] But who can imagine Paris without it today. And think of the twin towers of the World Trade Centre in Manhattan, once derisively referred to as the boxes in which the skyscrapers were packed, but with their tragic obliteration appreciated anew by many as beloved lost symbols of a city (or perhaps beloved symbols of a lost city).

It would be fascinating to know what pilgrims in 1149, viewing for the first time the extraordinary façade on the newly completed Church of the Holy Sepulchre in Jerusalem, thought of that eclectic creation.

It is not surprising that the most memorable church in the Latin East, perhaps indeed the most remarkable of all churches in the Christian World, should be that which the crusaders built to occupy the site that had motivated the First Crusade, and that lay at the very heart of Christian belief. The design of the new church was based on that of the European pilgrimage churches in France and Spain, and its decoration was largely in the European Romanesque style that was pre-

---

6 https://www.weekendnotes.com/shrine-of-remembrance./

7 Julian Green, *Paris*, bilingual edition, English translation by J. A. Underwood (1983; London: Boyars, 1991), 5.

Figure 7. Façade of the Church of the Holy Sepulchre.

dominant in western and central Europe at the time, but it also incorporated remnants of earlier Byzantine work and its structure and decoration included elements borrowed from or influenced by Muslim art. The southern façade was perhaps the least conventional façade of any church anywhere. It is exceptional both for its overall design, of which there are few parallels, and for the extraordinary diverse mix of decorative elements. The façade gives access to the church's southern transept, which, because of topographical and other restraints, was required to serve as the principal entrance to the church. As such it had to be both particularly splendid, and unique in its form and design. It is certainly both of these. In its overall layout, the façade consists of two horizontal registers; the ground floor level with two huge portals, and the upper level with two large windows that together with their external decoration are of equal size to the portals below, the two levels separated by a massive cornice. In its layout the façade bears some resemblance to that of the pilgrim church of Santiago de Compostela in northwest Spain, and it has been suggested that perhaps its design was also inspired by that of the Umayyad Golden Gate on the eastern wall of Jerusalem's Temple Mount.

Much indeed has been written about this façade. What I wish to note here is how the rather fantastic decorative elements somehow work and fit together, despite the extreme eclecticism. The decoration consists primarily of sculpture, although there had once also been glass mosaics in the tympanum. Among the sculptural elements are the two very fine carved lintels. These are also no longer *in situ* but can still be observed in the Rockefeller Museum to where they were removed in 1927. The western lintel, in the French Romanesque mode, displays scenes from the life of Jesus prior to the Crucifixion, including the Raising of Lazarus, the Entry into Jerusalem, and the Last Supper. The eastern lintel is in the Italian Romanesque style and displays a vine-scroll containing human and mythological figures. This use of two starkly different lintels over a single entrance is exceptional in church façades. Nonetheless, it does not appear at all incongruous. The entire façade with all its sculpture follows this same amalgam of oddly combined forms and styles. Yet somehow it works. There are eleven capitals around the doors, Byzantine/Romanesque in design, including the more standard acanthus leaf Corinthian type but also the less typical and perhaps local "windswept leaf" type. There is the Romanesque horizontal moulding that forms abaci over the capitals. One of the most noticed and noticeable features is the goudron hood moulding over the doors and windows. Popularly known for its form as "pillow" or "cushion arches" the goudron has often been regarded as being of Islamic origin, but more recently as having an Armenian or north Syrian origin.[8] Around these arches and extending horizontally as an additional moulding is a rosette frieze of sixth-century Syrian design, though now believed to be a twelfth-century work and not, as was suggested in the past, reused spolia. Very prominent in the façade are the heavy Roman style

---

8 Nurith Kenaan-Kedar, "Decorative Architectural Sculpture in Jerusalem: The Eastern, Western and Armenian Sources of a Local Visual Culture," in *The Crusader World*, ed. Adrian J. Boas (London: Routledge, 2016), 609–23 at 611.

cornice between the two levels and the beautiful European hood moulding of the upper windows with its floral motifs. In the very far eastern corner, at the entrance to a Coptic chapel and the stairway up to the monastic cloister, is a rather remarkable sculpture showing two lions, the presence of which seems almost an afterthought. It is the only figural element still to be seen on the façade.

The Holy Sepulchre façade is almost like an architect's model showcase or sampler, combining elements of pagan, early Christian, Byzantine, Armenian, Islamic, and European Romanesque design. There is nothing else quite like it. It is a sort of monumental triumphal arch, but an extraordinary one, somehow retaining its calm, majestic composure despite the almost chaotic details—the elaborate, deep-carved friezes, the different-coloured marble shafts, the complex swirling capitals, heavy classical cornices, bright mosaics, and multiple door and window arches. We might expect that the incongruity of its separate parts would produce a visual cacophony, but it does not. Perhaps it is simply that like the Shrine and the Eifel Tower, or like the bodily deformity of a close acquaintance, it has become so familiar to us that the dissonance is no longer noticed.

* * *

Today Jerusalem's walls have seven functioning gates (they had at least eleven in the Middle Ages). Some of these are named for places they lead towards—Zion Gate, Jaffa Gate, Damascus Gate, others for men, holy or otherwise—Herod's Gate and St. Stephen's Gate, the latter also named for a decorative feature it contains—Lions Gate, or simply for their age—New Gate. The one with the strangest, and, it would seem, most inappropriate name for a Holy City, is Dung Gate.

In his book *Mornings in Mexico*,[9] D. H. Lawrence gave an enlightening description of the tanning industry as carried out by the native Indians. He describes an encounter between

9 D. H. Lawrence, *Mornings in Mexico and Etruscan Places* (Harmondsworth: Penguin, 1960), 49–50.

himself (presumably) and a fat merchant of leather sandals and his wife, in which the couple regarded with high entertainment Lawrence's complaint of the distinct smell of a pair of sandals. The "leather man" claimed that there was no smell at all. Lawrence, realizing in retrospect that for the native there was indeed no perceivable smell, or rather that it was merely the smell of a sandal ("You might as well quarrel with an onion for smelling like an onion"), explains the likely reason for the odour, and the reason why the leather man and his wife did not even notice it. He writes that when the Spanish conquistador, Bernal Diaz del Castillo, came with Cortez to the great market of Mexico City, he saw rows of small pots of human excrement for sale and noted that the leather-makers who used it for tanning would sniff the different pots to see which was best. For these connoisseurs of excreta, what we regard as a particularly odious smell was perhaps quite an agreeable one.

Not only excrement, but urine as well was used to make leather hides pliable and enable the removal of hair. After initial treatment with urine, the hides were pounded or kneaded with the excrement. This technique was not unique to Mexico, though in many places it was not human waste that was used, but rather, and perhaps mildly less revoltingly, the dung of dogs or pigeons. It is here that lies the origin of the name of Jerusalem's Dung Gate, which is located in the southeast of the city, an area known in the past for the presence of leather works. Indeed, the connection between the name and the tanning industry is supported by the fact that just a few metres west of Dung Gate is another gate, a medieval one, long sealed and out of use and only recently excavated and reopened, and its medieval name was Tanners' Gate (*Porta Taneria*).

It is not difficult to understand why this industry and the accompanying cattle market and Street of the Furriers were delegated to a peripheral part of the city. The westerly winds would carry the unpleasant smells of the animals and the industry away into the desert. It was also a convenient location because of the excellent drainage and access to a good water source at the nearby Siloam Pool. When the industry did eventually move into the residential heart of the city during the Ottoman period, the reason seems to have been once again related to the unpleasant smell. This move was motivated by a desire to humiliate the Christian community, into whose neighbourhood the industry was now transplanted. A nineteenth-century photograph shows an open field directly in front of the entrance to the Church of the Holy Sepulchre, formerly part of the Hospitallers' compound, across which row after row of animal hides were laid out to dry. The move of the industry to this location gave substance to the derisive Arabic title for the Church of the Holy Sepulchre, which, at least as early as the twelfth century had been distorted from *Kanisat al-Qiyama* (Church of the Resurrection) to *Kanisat al-Qumama* (Church of the Dungheap).

Acre

Narrow alleys, twisting, climbing, sloping down towards the sea, steps rising out of long-buried houses, empty cul-de-sacs, weathered sandstone walls, patches of concrete, pale-blue plastered domes, towers, irregular-shaped stone-paved plazas, bins overflowing with garbage, filthy, half-starved cats, sewage trickling along open drains, a courtyard with some tombstones shaded by a fig tree, stairs rising up to a first and second storey, electricity wires looping between houses, a once fine merchant's house, now well past its hey-day, its windows sealed with concrete and corrugated iron, an empty warehouse with a dark, hardly visible interior of medieval vaulting, painted signs in Arabic and Hebrew calligraphy, a crowded suq of stalls selling fruit, fish, olive-oil soap, porcelain plates and jugs; pointed stone arches, broken windows, plastic shutters, pipes running obliquely across walls, walls that wear patches of plaster—patch on patch of past renovations and aborted improvements, fluttering laundry strung across a street, dirty children, the smell of cooking, oriental spices, aromatic coffee, a sickly scent of apple-flavoured tobacco from the nargileh shop, crooked cool passages hardly wide enough for a single person to pass, and the bay...oh, the bay, viewed between walls, stretching out like a great blue fan.

Figure 8. Aerial photograph of Akko.

What is it like to live in a town like this, a town that has grown haphazard over its past? Not easy, I would imagine. Today's Akko, despite some serious efforts to shake it out of its quagmire, is a town well and truly in decline. Perhaps this is because it is somehow unable to come to terms with the past. Despite all efforts, it remains in uneasy tension with its history. For its inhabitants, the once great city that lies buried beneath them is someone else's past. The people living here know little of its former splendour, though they cannot be entirely ignorant of it, for they are constantly encountering its relics. The lost city is not only beneath them. It surrounds them. It is in their streets, in their houses. Bits of it are incorporated into their rooms, the house facades, the courtyards. Its labyrinths intermingle with their labyrinths. They have settled over it in squalor. Their refuse is thrown down into its vaults, their sewage seeps down into its murky passageways. Its buried remains are warrens for rats and cockroaches. For today's inhabitants the past has its uses, but they are rather pitiful ones. The old halls and passages serve as convenient places to dispose of defunct refrigerators, old bedsteads, mattresses. Over the decades a butcher has dumped cattle bones here—gaunt, white, shoulder-high piles of ribs, vertebrae, and jawbones.

So, there are two cities: the city of the past and that of the present. In status they are worlds apart. Frankish Acre was the most vibrant and cosmopolitan town in the Levant. Its port rivalled the famed ports of Alexandria and Constantinople. But today's Akko is a drowsy, dirty, picturesque tourist town, its port is a tiny marina of fishing boats, no more substantial than that of any small fishing village. Modern Akko's origins lie in the eighteenth century, in a harbour town built by the Bedouin chieftain, Dahr al-Omar, to serve as an outlet for his cotton exports, earlier perhaps, its very beginnings being from when people first began to settle among the ruins of the crusader port in the fourteenth century. A seventeenth-century illustration shows masses of tiny houses already clustered, but dwarfed among the ruins of medieval palaces, churches, and great merchant houses.

* * *

Had there been such a thing as a Frankish Minister of Tourism of Acre, he would probably not have been on the best of terms with the caustic bishop, James of Vitry. James did a rather poor job in promoting his adopted city after he arrived there in 1216. He described it as being "like a monstrous dragon with nine heads engaged in mutual conflict." He referred to it as "a corrupt city...a second Babylon...full of innumerable crimes and iniquities." Murders took place in the open, night and day, husbands slit their wives' throats, if they were expeditious enough to do so before their wives beat them to it by dispatching them "in traditional fashion" with poison. There were drug traffickers, and people who concocted poisons from animal excrement. The city was full of brothels, and monks and priests happily hired out their lodgings to prostitutes.[10]

---

10 *Letters from the East: Crusades, Pilgrims and Settlers in the*

We might be excused in thinking that the bishop, always very forthcoming in his criticism, was doing a bit of embellishment, but there are others who shared his low opinion of the largest and most cosmopolitan metropolis in the Latin East. The papal legate Odo of Châteauroux, who was in Acre in the mid-thirteenth century, is quoted as saying "No one knows as well as I do of all the mean and treacherous sins committed in Acre." His was the somewhat brutal suggestion that the city needed to be "washed clean in the blood of its inhabitants."[11] If we wish to know why Acre had descended to such depths of iniquity, we can find the answer in the words of the Dominican friar, Burchard of Mount Sion (ca. 1274–1284) who records that Acre had become the dumping ground for Western murderers, robbers, thieves, and adulterers.[12] By the thirteenth century when these comments were made, Acre had truly evolved, as one observer commented, into a "new Sodom." And its moral filth had been accompanied by corporeal filth—pollution, which was seen as the cause of diseases and frequent deaths.

Having myself grown up in a country that started out as a dumping ground for murderers, robbers, thieves, and adulterers, I am less certain than perhaps those contemporary chroniclers would have been that Frankish Acre might not have had a positive future, had history played it a different set of cards. As for the pollution, that is something that is still very much present in Akko, but it is far from unique in that regard. Global maritime pollution has today reached catastrophic proportions. At Catania in Sicily in 2003, a report of the United Nations Environment Programme (UNEP) was released during the 13th meeting of the Barcelona Conven-

12th–13th Centuries, ed. and trans. Malcolm Barber and Keith Bate, Crusade Texts in Translation 18 (Farnham: Ashgate , 2013, 101–3.

11 Geoffrey Villehardouin, Jean de Joinville, *Chronicles of the Crusades*, trans. Frank Marzials (1908; Mineola: Dover, 2007), 250.

12 Burchardus de Monte Sion, *Descriptio Terrae Sanctae*, in *Peregrinatores medii aevi quattuor*, ed. J. C. M. Laurent (Leipzig: Hinrichs, 1864), 86–88.

tion for the protection of the Mediterranean Sea. It recorded for the first time the vast quantities of pesticides, heavy metals, and other pollutants that the surrounding countries have been dumping into the sea. These add to the massive quantities of solid debris, mainly plastics, that are having so disastrous an impact on wildlife today. It has been estimated that one hundred million tonnes of plastic have been dumped in the world's oceans, making up about eighty percent of the maritime debris that is turning our planet into a nightmare for future generations. Another claim that can drive home just how appalling this situation may be, is that by the year 2050 the oceans will contain more plastic than fish. The situation in the Mediterranean; a closed sea surrounded by major industrial nations, is particularly dire. It is estimated that it takes almost a full century for the water of the Mediterranean to be renewed. The huge increase in population of the surrounding countries, the vast expansion in industry over the past two centuries and the insufficient measures taken in the disposal of waste have made the problem of maritime pollution a critical one, threatening the continued survival of sea life, and indeed of life in general. But if the scale of this disaster is comparatively recent, the phenomenon, as we have noted, is not. In a study of various issues relating to Frankish Acre published in 1993, David Jacoby examined the occasional appearances in medieval sources relating to the city, of the term "*Lordemer*" (alternatively *Lordamer/Ordamer/Immundum*). Its meaning is "filthy sea." Jacoby identified this as referring to the city's port,[13] which is appropriate to what we know of medieval Acre and the pollution it experienced during the centuries of Frankish rule. The Greek pilgrim, Joannes Phocas (ca. 1185), described the crowded port city as suffering from "evil smells and corruption of the air" to the extent that "the misfortune of the city is beyond repair" and a contemporary Muslim visitor,

---

13 David Jacoby, "Three Notes on Crusader Acre," *Zeitschrift des Deutschen Palästina-Vereins* 109 (1993): 83–96 at 88–91.

Ibn Jubayr wrote that Acre "stinks and is filthy, being full of refuse and excrement."[14] Most of this filth ended up in the port. The slaughterhouse, butchers' stalls, and fish-sellers were located beside the port, and they added to the waste that flowed from the city's sewers into the harbour, including the sewage carried by a remarkable system of vaulted channels draining the Hospitallers' latrine tower. Being walled-in, with breakwaters and enclosing walls, the port retained this filth, churning around among the ships. In this, the port of Acre was like a miniature version of the Mediterranean, an enclosed space into which refuse was continually being dumped, and which, because of its comparatively small entrance, retained that filth, to the increasing detriment of those living in its vicinity. In the case of Acre, this ended when the city was destroyed in 1291. We must hope that the ominous condition of the Mediterranean will not likewise be resolved only by the destruction of the human presence that surrounds it.

* * *

After 1104 most merchants and pilgrims arriving in the Holy Land came ashore at the newly conquered port of Acre. It was not a particularly large harbour, and it had some serious problems, among these its above-mentioned use as a place to dispose of the city's considerable quantities of sewage. It was nonetheless the best harbour in the southern Levant, and under Frankish rule it became, after Constantinople and Alexandria, the busiest port in the eastern Mediterranean. During the *passagia* (the bi-annual sailing seasons) it was port of call to hosts of ships, and Theoderich, recorded that:

---

14 Joannes Phocas, *Descriptio Terrae Sanctae*, in *Description of the Holy Land / by John of Würzburg (A.D. 1160–1170)*, trans. Aubrey Stewart, Library of the Palestine Pilgrims' Text Society 5 (London: Palestine Pilgrims' Text Society, 1896), 11; Ibn Jubayr, *The Travels of Ibn Jubayr: A Medieval Journey from Cordoba to Jerusalem*, trans. R. J. C. Broadhurst (London: Cape, 1952), 318.

> ...on the Wednesday in Easter week we counted eighty ships in the port besides the ship called a "buss," on board of which we sailed thither and returned.[15]

The small size of the enclosed harbour was made up for by the fact that it was nestled in the large bay that extends between Acre in the north and the town of Haifa (Caifas) to the south. William of Tyre described Acre's port as "infra moenia et exterius" (within and beyond the walls)[16] which is sometimes interpreted as meaning that the ships were harboured within the breakwaters, walls, and chain of the port, but also outside in the open bay. That would certainly make it easier to see how eighty ships might anchor there on a single day. An alternative interpretation of William's words is suggested by the maps of Frankish Acre. Fourteenth-century maps, such as that drawn by the cartographers, Pietro Vesconte and Paolino Veneto seem to support the existence of a small, semi-circular basin extending into the city at the junction of the three Italian quarters.

If this is the case, the meaning of William's statement might be that those ships within the walls were harbouring in this inner basin and those outside the walls were in the larger enclosed area of the port. Most likely, perhaps, there were indeed all three anchorages in use during the *passagia*—the inner basin, perhaps for unloading of ships belonging to the Italian communes, the walled harbour for all other ships, and the open bay beyond for those waiting to dock or depart.

In the past, opposition has been raised regarding the existence of such an inner basin within the main harbour. In the 1960s, archaeologists excavated trenches inside the courtyard of the Khan al-Umdan, a large Turkish khan located at the southern end of the harbour near the breakwater. Khan

---

15 *Theoderich's Description of the Holy Places (circa 1172 A.D.)*, trans. Aubrey Stewart, Library of the Palestine Pilgrims' Text Society 5, no. 4 (London: Palestine Pilgrims' Text Society, 1891), 60.

16 William of Tyre, *Chronicon*, ed. Huygens, bk. 10, chap. 26; *Deeds*, ed. Babcock and Krey, 2:485.

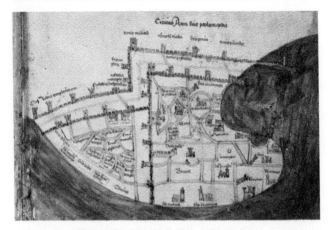

Figure 9. Pietro Vesconte's map of Acre, fourteenth century.
British Library, MS 27376, fols. 189v–190r.

al-Umdan has generally been regarded as being located on silted up land formerly occupied by the basin. The excavation, however, revealed that the khan courtyard had been constructed directly on bedrock, which seemed to rule out that possibility, and put a damper on the very existence of an inner basin.[17] As the basin nonetheless appears on the medieval maps, it was suggested that it might perhaps have been an invention of the cartographers? Medieval maps often contain as much invention as fact. The archaeologists suggested that, if not an invention, possibly it is the result of a cartographic error, an error caused by misinterpretation. Before the age of the printing press, illustrations in manuscripts, like the texts themselves, were copied by hand, usually by monks secreted away in the scriptoria of monasteries far from the locations described or illustrated. They used an existing illus-

---

17 Elisha Linder and Avner Raban, "Underwater Survey in the Harbour of Acre (1964)," in *Western Galilee and the Coast of Galilee* (Jerusalem: Israel Exploration Society, 1965), 193.

tration as the source for copying. Without personal acquaintance with the object they were drawing, if some details were unclear, they would copy what they believed they saw or understood, and they would also occasionally use their imaginations to make their versions appear more attractive or to give them a personal touch. As a result, we often find that when we have several versions of the same map, they are by and large similar, but vary in detail. Having failed to find the basin where they had supposed it to be, the archaeologists suggested that what appears as a basin on the maps may in fact have been the perpetuation on later copies of an accidental inkblot that had fallen onto the map as it was being prepared. A drop of green ink used to colour the sea fell perhaps from the pen, and later copiers believing it to be an actual feature copied it onto their versions.

The trouble with this proposal is that in more recent times, before Turkish Akko was built on top of the medieval ruins, the inner basin was actually observed by a number of people. It appears, for example, in 1799 on maps drawn by Colonel Jaquotin of Napoleon's army, as well as on several later French maps.[18] Indeed, as late as 1871 it was seen and described by the French archaeologist Emmanuel Rey, who noted that at that time it was filled with sand.[19] Rey is regarded as a very reliable authority. So, it would seem that there was indeed an inner harbour, and this was not a cartographer's misinterpretation, not a blot of green ink that fell from Vesconte's pen. Why then did the archaeologists not find it? The solution lies, I think, in the difficulty of interpreting the location of modern structures on medieval maps, with their obvious distortions and inaccuracies. The Khan al-Umdan appears to have been situated a little to the north of the medieval basin and the basin itself is no doubt buried beneath Ottoman structures just to its south.

* * *

18 Bernard Dichter, *The Maps of Acre. An Historical Cartography* (Acre: Municipality of Acre, 1973), 141.

19 Dichter, *The Maps of Acre*, 64–65.

Almost all the great buildings of Frankish Acre are lost. One of the most complete vanishing acts was that of the Templar palace, which stood at the southern end of the western shore. Its site is today occupied by a small and shallow basin, on a rock shelf surrounded by much deeper water. There are a few insubstantial remains of its foundation walls preserved to a height of about 70 cm, entirely submerged today beneath the sea, which in the past eight centuries has risen nearly one and a half metres above its level in the Middle Ages. These fragments are all that remains of what appears to have been the most splendid, prominent, and probably the strongest building of Frankish Acre. The Templar compound included not only the palace, but also a church, two towers, and various other buildings. The German pilgrim Theoderich (ca. 1169) referred to this palace as "a house of huge and wonderful workmanship on the seashore,"[20] but the most detailed description of it dates to about 120 years later, in a text known simply as *The Templar of Tyre*, which describes the city at the time of its fall in May 1291, and refers to the Templar palace as "the strongest place in the city":

> It occupied a large site on the sea, like a castle; it had at its entry a tall, strong tower, and the wall was thick, 28 feet wide. On each corner of the tower was a turret, and upon each turret was a gilded lion passant, as big as a donkey,... and it was the most magnificent thing to see."[21]

The chronicler goes on to describe a corner tower, the master's palace, and other buildings including a second tower located "so close to the sea that the waves broke against it." This latter tower dated from the brief period of Ayyubid rule in Acre between 1187 and 1191 and it was said to have been built by Saladin himself. The Templars subsequently used it as a stronghold for their treasury.

---

20 *Theoderich's Description of the Holy Places*, trans. Stewart, 59.

21 *The Templar of Tyre: The Deeds of the Cypriots*, trans. Paul Crawford, Crusade Texts in Translation 6 (Aldershot: Ashgate, 2003, 114.

The strength of the Templars' main tower enabled it to hold out for several days after the rest of the city capitulated to the Mamluks on May 15, 1291. It fell only on the 28th after it had been undermined. In a dramatic description of this, the Templar of Tyre writes of how the Mamluks dug a mine under the tower. Upon observing this, the defenders surrendered, but although the miners had shored it up, so many of the Mamluks had already entered that the supports gave way and the tower collapsed. The attackers were killed together with the Franks as it crashed out into the adjacent street, where he notes, probably with considerable exaggeration, an additional two thousand mounted Mamluks were crushed to death.[22] The fall of the palace signalled the end of resistance, the end of Frankish Acre, and indeed, the end of the kingdom of Jerusalem.

The remains of the palace and other buildings (apart from an impressive tunnel that gave the Templars a private route from their palace to the port) are so scanty that it is impossible today to get any sense of what they had originally looked like. Contemporary and near-contemporary illustrations appear on maps, but they are symbolic rather than realistic renditions, and cannot at all be relied upon. The very thorough dismantling by the Mamluks that followed the conquest and occupation of the city in 1291 must have left this splendid palace and the other Templar buildings in a complete state of ruin. But, like other substantial monuments of Frankish Acre, being such a monumental structure, a considerable part of it appears to have continued standing in a ruined state for several hundred years. An illustration purportedly showing the ruins of the palace and church as they appeared in 1748, was published by Ladislaus Mayr, a Franciscan from Bavaria, in 1781. A caption on the engraving states in German that the buildings had been demolished in 1752. The remains illustrated appear to have been quite extensive. If indeed it does represent the ruins of the Templar palace (for despite the very explicit caption, this identification has recently been contested), it is the only visual representation we have of

---

22 *The Templar of Tyre*, trans. Crawford, 117.

what was certainly one of the most remarkable architectural creations of the Crusader period.

The Countryside

A "monadnock," to use the Native American term, or "insel-berg," island mountain in German, its isolation makes the dome-shaped Mount Tabor stand out so prominently. To its north and east are the low hills of the Nazareth Range and to the south, extending west towards the coast, is the broad sweep of the Jezreel Valley, the Plain of Esdraelon. So spherical is its form, it might be a great bubble that has risen from the earth's molten core and is pushing through the crust, about to burst over the silent fields and olive groves. And how Biblical a feature in a landscape where geology and theology play together on our perceptions. The Hebrew name, Tavor (תבור) has been regarded as etymologically connected to the Hebrew word tabbur (טבור) meaning "navel." There is no real basis for this, and that particular association is usually reserved in this holy landscape for Jerusalem, which on the medieval mappa mundi is the *umbilicus* of the world; but an anatomical and birth-related association certainly does go hand-in-hand with the mountain's breast-like form.

I have only been up once, a number of years ago, which is quite remarkable for it being so prominent and frequently seen from a distance. I drove with an archaeologist friend on the steep road that winds up its side like a spiralling ribbon through the pine forest. The forest itself is new, the usual reforestation in orderly rows that covers a fair part of the sides and ends in a straight line, as if the Zionist planters had got just that far when the money ran out. In the twelfth century the slopes were dressed in cultivated trees and the pilgrim, abbot Daniel of Kiev, who visited in 1105/6 wrote: "Mount Tabor is all covered with trees of every kind, figs and carobs and olives in great abundance," but by the late nineteenth century when the French photographer Félix Bonfils took his beautiful photograph of it, all of this was gone, and the mountain was bald. At the top there were only ruins of

Figure 10. Mount Tabor.

the medieval defences and remnants of the Byzantine and Frankish chapels.

In the Book of Joshua (19:22) Mount Tabor is a landmark for identifying the border of the tribes of Zebulun, Issachar, and Naphtali. During the Jewish revolt against Rome in 66 AD the summit of the mountain was fortified and defended by the military governor of the Galilee, later turncoat and historian, Yosef ben Matityahu/Josephus Flavius, who referred to it in his *Jewish War* by the name Itabryon. It fell to Vespasian the following year. Since the third or perhaps fourth century, Tabor has been identified as the Mount of Transfiguration.

As early as 1101, a Benedictine fortified abbey was built on the mountain top. It was subsequently refortified by the Franks who saw the strategic value in its prominence and in that it overlooked the Damascus road at the place where it passed into the Jezreel Valley. William of Tyre records that during Saladin's raid into the Galilee in 1182, the Ayyubids arrived at the village of Buria, today's Daburia, at the foot of Tabor, a faubourg dependent on the fortified abbey.[23]

---

23 William of Tyre, *Chronicon*, ed. Huygens, bk. 22, chap. 14; *Deeds*, ed. Babcock and Krey, 2:469–70.

The unprepared villagers fled to their tower but within four hours the Muslims managed to undermine it and many of the Franks were killed. During this raid, the Muslims took away five hundred prisoners of war. Saladin invaded again the following year and, as they would fatefully do so again a few years later, the Frankish troops gathered at the Springs of Sephorie. On realizing that the Ayyubids had taken control of the region of Beisan (Bet She'an) to the east, the Franks moved their troops via the Nazareth mountains and down into the Plain of Esdraelon. In reaction Saladin's troops broke camp and scattered about, ravaging the countryside, and some climbed Mount Tabor, but the monks and villagers who had taken refuge in the monastery managed to hold out, a tribute to the strength of the fortifications by that time.[24] After the Battle of Hattin, Sultan Al-Adil, refortified the mountain with strong new walls, considerable sections of which can still be observed.

Not everyone is "transfigured" by Tabor. Mark Twain in a rather disparaging shade on his typical droll style, was unimpressed by the ruins at Tabor:

> There is nothing for it now but to come back to old Tabor, though the subject is tiresome enough, and I cannot stick to it for wandering off to scenes that are pleasanter to remember.

He seems to have found positive words only for the coffee he was given at the Greek convent. Of the antiquities that he saw, so he writes, there was nothing but "...some old grey ruins" and he was disappointed by the fact that he could observe "never a splinter of the true cross or bone of a hallowed saint to arrest the idle thoughts of worldlings and turn them into graver channels."[25] But it was the mountain top and expectations of some remarkable remains that disappointed Twain, not the mountain itself, of which he was rather more admiring, describing it as:

---

24 William of Tyre, *Chronicon*, ed. Huygens, bk. 22, chap. 26; *Deeds*, ed. Babcock and Krey, 2:495.

25 Chap. 49 of Mark Twain, *The Innocents Abroad* (Hartford: American, 1869), 520, 523, 534.

...symmetrical and full of grace—a prominent landmark, and one that is exceedingly pleasant to eyes surfeited with the repulsive monotony of desert Syria.

* * *

There is something about human resilience that has to be admired, even when it is entirely irrational. Anyone who has lived in a war zone has witnessed how, as long as it is possible, and often when it appears not to be, people go about their daily lives while the world is crumbling around them. It is precisely this quality that enables cities to thrive on the slopes of volcanoes or along geological faults, on the edge of creeping desert dunes or behind dikes holding back the peril of the sea. But danger is not limited to war zones or the edges of volcanoes. It is part of human existence, even in the most docile of surroundings. From early on we learn the ability to get on with our lives regardless of what may be lurking around the corner. Sometimes, for the immediate fulfilment of our desires or for the thrill of living on the edge, we even promote danger by rash behaviour such as extreme sports, smoking, over-eating, or driving irresponsibly.

There was a period of a few decades in the twelfth century when the Christian settlers in the crusader states lulled themselves into an imprudent and entirely false sense of security. There was nothing to support this: no decline in the rhetoric or intentions of their neighbours. Yet the Franks were suddenly feeling very confident. For several decades they had been careful not to expose themselves to danger and had settled exclusively behind city fortifications or within strongly defended fortresses. But in the 1140s this began to change, increasingly so in after 1153. In that year, Ascalon, the one coastal city in Latin territory that had remained in Muslim hands after the occupation of Tyre in 1124, and the most active threat to the internal security of the kingdom, was finally occupied. Its conquest was like the removal of a bothersome thorn. It had been the source of continual raids into the heart of the kingdom and had kept the settlers in a perpetual state of siege.

Now there was a change in the mindset of the settlers. The border had seemingly moved back towards the desert. Egypt seemed so much further away, and a movement of settlement activity began outside the protective embrace of city walls. By the 1160s Frankish rural settlement in the hills around Jerusalem was in full swing. Indeed, it was so intensive that on almost every hill and in every valley around the city one can still observe today the remains of Frankish villages, farms, estate centres, and agricultural installations.

Aqua Bella compellingly illustrates how the settlers wholly embraced what was fundamentally an unwarranted confidence in the internal security of the kingdom. This large, rural administrative centre, west of Jerusalem on the road to Jaffa, was built without fortified elements, and with half of its ground floor excavated deep into the side of a hill, a position that left it particularly vulnerable if an enemy were to approach it from that side.

It seems that the Hospitaller owners of this building did not conceive of assault as a likely occurrence. This misplaced faith in their security was repeated and can be observed in many other rural sites. One notable example is in the adoption by landowners like the canons of the Church of the Holy Sepulchre, and perhaps by others as well, of the European "street-village" design for the settlements that they had begun to establish in the countryside around Jerusalem. The layout of these villages with single rows of houses either side of a single street was, because of its narrow, elongated form, extremely difficult to defend. On a small hill rising to the right of the road that leads northwest from Jerusalem are the remains of one of these twelfth-century villages. Half hidden in the long grass and low bushes are numerous stone walls, remnants of the small houses that lined either side of the old Roman road, the *vicis ad civitatem*, that appears of the twelfth-century maps leading from nearby Montjoie (Nebi Samwil) to David's Gate. This is el-Kurum, the Vineyards. That is the name that these ruins have gone by since perhaps the Ayyubid period when the village was abandoned. The Frankish name is lost, but the association

Figure 11. Hospitaller rural estate centre, Aqua Bella.

with vineyards is evidenced in the presence of several wine presses located within a number of the ruined houses. Perhaps the conquering Ayyubids retained these vineyards, despite a decline in the wine industry under Muslim rule. Today, the Jerusalem suburb of Ramot has encroached and surrounded the hill, and a branch of the modern highway has cut through the edge of the long-abandoned village fields that can now only be made out by the terrace walls that divided them.

In 1992, a wave of immigration to Israel from the former Soviet Union resulted in a building boom and this hill was designated for the construction of a new housing project. At the top of the hill stand the remains of a medieval tower known as al-Joz (the Walnut). Around it are signs of other ancient structures, and the Israel Antiquities Authority carried out excavations here to determine whether the site was worthy of preservation or could be released for construction. After some weeks it was decided to permit the building to go ahead. Bulldozers were brought in and began work on one side of the site. However, on the very last day of excavations, one of the archaeologists noticed that further down the hill on the east were several ancient walls. The bulldozers were ordered to cease work, and a few weeks of excavations commenced, exposing the remains of about a dozen houses of the village. Two years later, I, myself, excavated some additional houses.

What we uncovered was just a small section of a type of settlement prevalent in medieval Europe but entirely unknown in the Middle East prior to the twelfth century. In the West, street-villages were one of the settlement types that evolved to cope with the great increase in population, an outcome of the medieval agricultural revolution. Settlements of this type, consisting of single rows of houses and agricultural plots either side of a street, were easy to set up and easy to administer. For that reason, this layout was regarded as an expedient form for the settlement that had began to pick up in the countryside around Jerusalem in the mid-twelfth century. The remains of five such villages are known today, all within the vicinity of Jerusalem. In setting up these villages between the 1140s and 1180s, the Franks retained the layout applied in European villages, dividing the land among the settlers in approximately equal portions. Each settler received a plot adjacent to the street on which to construct a house, and beyond the house a field, the same width as the house but extending far back. This latter plot, known as a "croft," was intended for the growing of crops and the raising of livestock. The plot for the construction of the house was referred to as a "toft." The medieval landowners were precise in formalizing both the obligations of peasants and the possessions granted to them, and details of these are preserved in surviving documents that describe the setting up of villages. In the West, where feudalism was more restrictive and peasants were of serf status, obligations were often severe. This is illustrated in the witticism: "The croft is a piece of land surrounded by regulations." In the Latin East the peasants were free settlers, and conditions were more relaxed. Nonetheless, we find a clear outline of what was granted. In terms of landed property this was a plot measuring two *carrucae* (the carruca being a measure of ploughland based on the estimated land that could be ploughed by a team of oxen in one day).[26]

All this has been much discussed. What has been less noticed is that the toft, as introduced in the Latin East became, perhaps for the first time, entirely occupied by the house rather than, as in contemporary Europe, the house being built within it. Houses were constructed, not as individual units as in the West, but with shared walls, those at the front and back of the plot often shared with several adjacent houses. Unlike their contemporaries in the West, but like the terrace houses of a later era, they were multi-unit constructions set up in a single effort, and as such they throw some light on the way new villages in the Latin East were established and constructed as communal endeavours.

Were the Frankish landowners burying their heads in the sand when building these undefended and indefensible buildings and settlements, or did they genuinely believe that, with the occupation of Ascalon and other measures taken, the threat to their presence in the Levant had been largely resolved? Having once observed people sunbathing at a beach resort, only a short distance from a battle in full swing and returning to my earlier allusion to cities on the edge of volcanoes, I tend to think the former. Either way, the bubble burst in 1187.

---

26 See, for example, the discussion in Ronnie Ellenblum, *Frankish Rural Settlement in the Latin Kingdom of Jerusalem* (Cambridge: Cambridge University Press, 1998), 97–99. See also Adrian J. Boas, *Crusader Archaeology. The Material Culture of the Latin East*, 2nd ed. (London: Routledge, 2017), 67–68.

Chapter 3

People

I love mankind...it's people I can't stand!!
Charles M. Schulz

Guy de Lusignan

Guy de Lusignan is perhaps the ultimate anti-hero of the crusader period. A Poitevin nobleman who became king of Jerusalem, he played what many regard as the principal role in the decline and eventual fall of the kingdom. Guy's story is an ill-fated one, but with a not entirely unfortunate ending. Some leaders suffer devastating defeats but are eventually able to recover their reputation. When Churchill was held responsible for the failure at Gallipoli in 1915, he was demoted from his position as First Lord of the Admiralty. He spent the remainder of the war years on the Western Front, where he commanded an infantry battalion, and after the war he began a long and slow recovery of his reputation until his complete rehabilitation as the leader of Britain in the Second World War. For Guy, even had he been as astute and well-regarded as Churchill, which he certainly was not, the shadow of the defeat at Hattin was so heavy and his role in it so indisputable, that his reputation, such as it was, was forever tainted. So much so that we tend to forget that after that defeat, he played a significant part in the recovery of the kingdom, enabling it to survive for another century. No less significant was the fact that he went on to establish a dynasty on the island of Cyprus that would carry his name and enable a crusader presence to survive in the Latin East for two centuries after the fall of Acre.

Guy faced criticism well before the Battle of Hattin. William of Tyre refers to him as "an obscure man, wholly incapable and indiscreet."[1] In stating this, the chronicler was ostensibly repeating the opinion of Guy's opponents, but clearly he was also expressing his own view. The very last words in the archbishop of Tyre's chronicle record Guy's repudiation by Baldwin IV after increasing acts of disobedience. These led the king to try to annul Guy's marriage to his sister Sibylla, and finally to place the regency of the kingdom and guardianship of his joint ruler, the child Baldwin V, in the hands of Guy's rival, Raymond III of Tripoli. Later, as king, Guy comes across the pages of history as feeble and indecisive, a man who acts out of weakness rather than strength. His conduct appears to have incited dissension and disunity at the most critical moment in crusader history, at the time when the kingdom was in its greatest need of unifying leadership. It cannot be denied that he bears much of the responsibility for the outcome of the Battle of Hattin. His decision, following a war council on July 2, 1187, to leave the comparative security at the Springs of Saforie and advance towards Tiberias, and ultimately into the waiting arms of Saladin's army below the Horns of Hattin, was in opposition to the long-established strategy of the Franks of avoiding open conflict with a numerically superior enemy. He is said to have been motivated in this by a desire to shake off the reputation he had gained in his mishandling of Saladin's invasion of 1183, during which he directed the largest field army ever assembled by the Franks. In that instance, although there was ample opportunity, Guy did not take the initiative and attack Saladin's troops, and did not make sufficient efforts to provide the army with supplies. Already regarded as being inexperienced, Guy proved himself to be irresolute as well.

---

1 William of Tyre, *Chronicon*, ed. Huygens, bk. 22, chap. 27; *Deeds*, ed. Babcock and Krey, 2:497.

Should all the blame fall on his shoulders? To be fair, in 1183 there were mitigating circumstances. Guy could not rely on the support of the other lords, for they refused to cooperate with him, out of fear that if the campaign were to be a success his position in the kingdom would be unassailable. But the end-result was that Guy gained the reputation of being an indecisive leader, and this certainly influenced his decision-making in the summer of 1187. A strong leader must take calculated risks when necessary, always with the good of his people foremost in mind, while a weak leader will allow his decisions to be influenced by his own fears of failure, and his principal concern is always his own reputation.

The outcome at Hattin was the utter defeat of the Frankish army and the subsequent loss of almost the entire kingdom, including the Holy City of Jerusalem. And although it was not to spell the immediate end of the crusading enterprise, it was a debacle that set the Franks on a downward trajectory. The kingdom would survive for another century thanks to a concerted effort of Western leaders in 1189–1191 (the Third Crusade) and somewhat less concerted and sporadic, but nonetheless significant, efforts of crusaders in the thirteenth century. The end finally came with the fall of Acre in May 1291.

Guy had arrived in the East sometime between 1173 and 1180, possibly with the French Crusaders of 1179. His older brother Aimery had paved the way for him to enter court circles, having himself married Eschiva, the daughter of the lord of Ibelin, and by obtaining the patronage of Baldwin IV. Guy's hasty marriage to the king's sister, Sibylla in April 1180, forestalled political manoeuvring by Raymond and Bohemond III of Antioch. As a result, Guy was elevated to the positions of Count of Jaffa and Ascalon and bailiff of Jerusalem. In 1182, when the king's leprosy blinded him and made him unable to walk, Guy was assigned the regency of the kingdom. In 1183 the king had his five-year-old nephew appointed as co-ruler, and after the Baldwin's death in 1185 Baldwin V ruled for a year under Raymond's regency until he also died. When Sibylla, who in order to become queen had agreed to annul her marriage to Guy, was crowned as queen regnant by the patriarch of Jerusalem, in a clever move that outwitted the opposition, she chose Guy once again as her husband, upon which he crowned himself king in the Church of the Holy Sepulchre.

Regarding the disastrous affair at Hattin, the question that we need to ask is: to what degree, beyond personal motivations, was Guy taking into account the risk he was placing on his army and indeed on the entire kingdom? The rift between the so-called "court faction" of Guy, Sibylla, the Templar Master, Gerard of Ridefort, and Raynald of Châtillon and the "nobles' faction" led by Raymond, meant that any decision made by Guy would be open to harsh criticism while any opposing suggestion by Raymond and the Hospitallers would equally be regarded as suspicious by the other side. At the war council held after Saladin laid siege to Tiberias on July 2, 1187, Raymond argued strongly against engaging in battle with the Muslims, and Gerard of Ridefort was equally vehement in favour of advancing against Saladin. Although Raymond's arguments were sound and in accordance with the usual Frankish strategy of avoiding direct confrontation, in particular when the odds were so obviously favourable to the Muslims, Guy chose to follow the advice of the Templar Master. The chronicler, Ernoul gives an account of Gerard's argument, and it fully exposes on the one hand the mistrust Guy had of Raymond, and on the other, how the Templar Master played upon Guy's fears of failure:

> Lord, do not believe the advice of the count. For he is a traitor, and you well know that he has no love for you, and wishes you to be shamed, and that you should lose the kingdom. But I counsel you to start out immediately, and we with you, and thereby overcome Saladin. For this is the first crisis that you have faced in your reign. If you do not leave this pasturage, Saladin will come and attack you here. And if you retreat from his attack the shame and reproach will be very great.[2]

---

2 Quoted in Malcolm Barber, *The New Knighthood. A History of the Order of the Temple* (Cambridge: Cambridge University Press, 1994, 112.

When Guy took the disastrous course of following Gerard's advice, he did so in an apparent effort to prove that he was capable of decisive action, but he only ended up exposing his irresolution. Had the battle been a Frankish success, history would undoubtedly have judged him differently. But Guy had failed in more than battle. His personal inadequacies were of such magnitude that he appears to have been willing to endanger the entire kingdom and the lives of many of his people to protect his own reputation.

So where can we find Guy's saving grace? At Hattin Guy was taken prisoner by Saladin and was later held in captivity in Damascus. He was finally granted release in 1188 and then sought refuge in Tyre, but was denied entry by Conrad of Montferrat, the Italian noble who at the time was leading the defence of the city. It was now that Guy began at last to act like a king. He turned south and opened the siege of Acre in anticipation of the arrival of the armies of the Third Crusade. It was this siege that eventually turned the tables and enabled the recovery of the coast and part of the former lands of the kingdom. Ultimately his army was joined by the French and English armies and remnants of the German forces, and under the leadership of Richard I of England and Philip Louis of France the tide turned in favour of the Christians. But Guy was about to face a new disaster. In the summer of 1190, during an epidemic in the crusader camp outside the walls of the city, Sibylla died. Guy no longer had a legitimate claim to the Jerusalem throne. But if he had lost of his kingdom, not all was lost. He was able to obtain another lordship in 1192 by purchasing the recently captured island of Cyprus. This was a certain compensation for the loss of Jerusalem, and it had long-lasting effects. When he died in 1194, he was succeeded by his brother Amalric who became the first king of Cyprus. The House of Lusignan was established and would survive until 1474.

So, if there is to be redemption for Guy in the pages of history it can be found in these later, post-Hattin events—in the role that he played rallying the Frankish army at Acre in 1189 and in the establishment of a new dynasty and a new kingdom in Cyprus. These saving graces enabled the Franks to retain a presence in the Levant that would survive for another two centuries after Acre finally fell in 1291. In short, we might say that it was Guy who played a substantial role in extending the crusading era for three hundred years, no small achievement and one that, had he not been responsible for nearly losing it in the first place, might have gained for him a rather better place in the history books.

Marino Sanudo

My mother, thin and frail in her old age, though never frail of mind, passed away at the age of 89, after a brief but painful battle with intestinal cancer. By the time of her death, she no longer had the ability to take food or drink, and she was in extreme pain that was only partly relieved by morphine. On the morning of her death, it was something of a relief to find that during the night she had fallen into a coma. Her departure towards midday was a release for her, though an immense sorrow that, for me, my younger brother, and my aunt who were present, was to be briefly followed by an additional and unanticipated trauma. Paramedics arrived, lifted her weightless body from the bed onto the floor, and, removing her wedding ring, proceeded in making a vigorous attempt at reviving her. They were of course merely doing their job, but it was not only a pointless endeavour; it was a painful and offensive one for us, and it has remained among the more indelible memories of that very sad day. When the end is inevitable, efforts at prolonging it can be not only futile, but cruel.

In 1271 the crusader states were in an advanced state of decay. That year the Mamluk Sultan Baibars occupied two of the great military order fortresses that provided a critical defensive line for Tripoli—Chastel Blanc (Safita), a prominent Templar keep surrounded by a fortified enclosure, and the great Hospitaller fortress, Crac des Chevaliers. Shortly afterward he took and dismantled the principal Teutonic fortress, Montfort in the western Galilee. The remaining coastal cities of the rapidly disintegrating crusader states were now entirely exposed, and the last of them, including the main surviving city, Acre, would fall two decades later. In the same year, the archdeacon of Liege, Teobaldo Visconti was participating in the Ninth Crusade and arrived at Acre accompanying Edward, the prince of Wales (later Edward I of England). On September 1, in his absence, Visconti was elected pope by the College of Cardinals meeting in Viterbo. His conversance with the situation in the Holy Land led the new pope, now Gregory X, as one of his first acts, to send out an appeal for aid for the crusaders. The response was almost complete apathy, and it appeared that the crusading movement had, at long last, run out of steam. It had been coming under increasing criticism for having abandoned spiritual motivation in favour of financial gain, and Gregory's efforts to turn the tables had little effect. A papal council was held at Lyon in 1274, and other efforts were made at stirring up renewed enthusiasm among European leaders and the heads of the military orders. James I of Aragon expressed his support for the immediate commencement of a crusade, plans were drawn up, and a decision was reached to raise finances with a six-year tithe. But all of this came to nothing. The proposal was opposed by the Templars, and it was not sufficiently supported by the attending representatives of the kings of Germany, England, Scotland, France, Iberia, and Sicily. There was simply no longer any enthusiasm for the idea, and the French ambassador to the papal court is said to have compared the plans for a renewed crusade to a small puppy barking at a large dog.[3] When, two decades after Gregory's election, the last Christian strongholds in Syria fell to the Mamluks, the idea of recovery seemed to be finally put to rest.

But there were still some who found this hard to accept. One of these was a Venetian named Marino Sanudo Torsello (ca. 1270–ca. 1334). Known today by the appellation Il Vecchio (the Elder) to distinguish him from a famous fifteenth to six-

---

3 Hans E. Mayer, *The Crusades*, 2nd ed. (Oxford: Oxford University Press, 1988), 282–83.

teenth-century historian and diarist known as Marino Sanudo the Younger, Sanudo was the son of a patrician of Venice. He had an ambitious plan for a renewed crusade to recover the mainland crusader states. It too would come to nothing, and historian Jonathan Riley-Smith coined for it the title *A Crusade that Never Was*.[4] It was nonetheless an impressive attempt. Sanudo carefully thought out and prepared a comprehensive and highly detailed proposal, that involved sending an advance naval expeditionary force to blockade Egypt, followed by a traditional, large crusading army. Through the combination of military force and an economic embargo he hoped to weaken and neutralize the Mamluks. And in truth it was a feasible idea. Had it not been for the fact that no one was interested any more, it might have succeeded.

In 1285, just six years before the fall of Acre, Sanudo visited the crusader port city where his family had commercial interests. Later, after the loss of the Holy Land in 1291, he travelled extensively through those parts of the eastern Mediterranean still under Christian rule. After composing his treatise, he presented it to Pope John XXII at Avignon in September 1321, under the title—*Liber secretorum fidelium crucis* (The Book of the Secrets of the Faithful of the Cross). The pope was an exceptional administrator who had taken great strides in reorganizing the Church, but sadly for Sanudo he was no Urban II, and this was not 1095. He appointed a commission to deliberate on Sanudo's proposal, but it was probably merely a charade, for he was no doubt aware that there was no wind left in the sails of the crusading movement. Sanudo was paid a handsome gratuity and was warmly praised, but his plan was shelved, to gather dust in the archives of the Vatican. For the remaining years of his life he continued, in correspondence with Western leaders, to push his plan, but to no avail. They were too deeply involved in domestic matters and were reluctant to support the vast cost of the project, which had been estimated by Sanudo at

---

4 Jonathan Riley-Smith, *The Atlas of the Crusades* (London: Times Books, 1991), 122–23.

210,000 gold florins. Indeed, interest in a new crusade had been buried even before Sanudo had written his treatise. By the time the Hospitallers occupied Rhodes (1306–1310), thoughts of recovering the East had been replaced by reduced and more realistic enterprises. In the words of historian Anthony Luttrell:

> The move to Rhodes almost suggests that the Hospitallers, having acknowledged the general renunciation of Jerusalem as a practical goal, had shrewdly anticipated the transformation of the crusade into a defensive struggle against the Turks. Latin society, in which an esprit laïque was increasingly strong, was turning not only against the papacy but also against the crusade which too often seemed to be a papal instrument exploited largely for political ends.[5]

The time had come, it would seem, to stop beating a dead horse. But, if Sanudo failed to arouse an interest in his project, if the world had moved on, and those still supporting the crusading movement were forced to accept that it was indeed beyond resuscitation, we can nonetheless be grateful for what this Venetian did achieve. For if there is a lasting value in his efforts, it is in his thorough research, in the extensiveness and detail he gave when itemizing what would be required for a crusade, such as weapons, ships, food, horses, people. And we can be grateful for the accompanying cartography, with which he illustrated his texts. Sanudo employed a mapmaker, probably the very able Genoese cartographer and geographer, Pietro Vesconte, who at that time was working in Venice. To accompany the texts, he prepared detailed and highly informative maps of the Middle East and Mediterranean, the Holy Land, Jerusalem, and perhaps most importantly from our point of view, the city of Acre. The Acre

---

5 Anthony Luttrell, "The Hospitallers of Rhodes: Prospectives, Problems, Possibilities," in Antony T. Luttrell, *Latin Greece, the Hospitallers and the Crusades, 1291–1440* (London: Variorum, 1982), 252; repr. from *Die geistlichen Ritterorden Europas*, ed. Josef Fleckenstein and Manfred (Sigmaringen: Thorbecke, 1980), 243–66.

map, in the particulars of which his own acquaintance with the city appears to be demonstrated, is a godsend for our understanding of this thirteenth-century port city. It provides us with information on the city's overall form, its internal lay-out, its numerous quarters and their names, and its principal institutions. On the basis of diverse renditions of this map (for, as with all medieval maps, there are a number of copies, with slight variances between them) historians and archaeol-ogists have been able to reconstruct the city at its peak, to locate and identify, despite obvious inaccuracies and distor-tions, the names, boundaries, components, occupants, and functions of the quarters, the routes of the principal roads, the layout of the military order compounds, and the positions of the fortifications (including the locations and even the names of the gates, towers, and moats).

So, if the crusader movement was dead and relegated to the pages of the history books, Sanudo's careful planning and recording has, at the very least, contributed to the historians' efforts in understanding and interpreting what had been lost. One might almost say that Sanudo was successful, if not in bringing about his crusade and recovering a Latin East, at least in preserving it in our minds.

Germain

Melbourne, the city where I grew up, is well known for its highly changeable weather. I recall as a child going with a close friend and his family to the beach on a hot mid-sum-mer morning. We left the car and ran barefoot across the already searing asphalt and the even more blistering sand to the water's edge, where we played in the sea for some time until, quite suddenly, a very strong wind picked up and the temperature plummeted. The wind was indeed so strong that when we tossed our towels in the air it lifted them up and carried them a fair way, and we enjoyed this game for a few minutes until it became altogether too cold and windy, and heavy, fat drops of rain began to fall. Then we ran for cover, and back to the car, and I recall the strange sensation of it having become cold so rapidly that the sand and asphalt were still quite hot, and we could hardly sit on the car seats.

One of the chief difficulties I faced in acclimatizing, when my family emigrated to Israel, was the weather (an interesting term—"acclimatizing"—pointing to the fact that climate is indeed one of the more difficult things to adjust to). Having been used to the changeability of Melbourne weather, I found the Mediterranean summer to be overly constant. In the Middle East, summer is well and truly the dominant season. The main distinction between it and the seasons that precede and follow is that, while summer is unendurably long and predictable, both the spring and the autumn seasons are highly variable and fleeting transitions. Other than the delightful but all too brief springtime activities of the flora and fauna, and the equally brief and, compared to some other parts of the world, decidedly modest colour-changing spectacle of the deciduous trees, one might be inclined to think there are only two seasons here—a volatile but rather short-lived winter and a long-enduring and fatiguing summer. People who have been born here are quite used to this, but when I first encountered it, I felt as if there was no weather here at all. It was simply always hot. Because of this, and because other aspects of life are so much more capricious, in the Middle East weather is only a topic of discussion on occasions when it does indeed behave less predictably. In most years such events rarely amount to more days than can be counted on one hand. Of late, however, global warming and the impact of extreme climatic events worldwide has made this part of the world, at least from that aspect, somewhat more normal. We are beginning to experience "more" weather; that is, more extreme temperatures, stronger winds, heavier and more intense rainfalls, and perhaps most unfortunately, more extended periods of drought.

Drought has always been part of the climatic cycle. With the rapid growth in population and the consequentially increased use of water resources for drinking, agriculture, and industry, the effects of drought have become a growing concern. New solutions have been sought, and modern technology has enabled the transformation of sea water into drinking water. In a sort of modern-day alchemy, a technology has even been developed for extracting water from air—in most regions of the world one square kilometre of atmospheric air is said to contain 10,000 to 30,000 cubic metres of pure water). In Israel, a few years ago, a large-scale desalination program was introduced. If it has not yet resolved the problem, it has certainly alleviated the effects of drought on the household water supply.

But there is a simpler method that has not been fully taken advantage of—a more effective harvesting of what comes naturally: rainwater. The short and intensive manner in which rain falls in arid and semi-arid regions does not enable the ground to effectively absorb the water, and the result is runoff of this valuable commodity, flowing away uselessly into the sea. I once observed this very dramatically when flying above the Mediterranean coast shortly after a heavy rainstorm. One could see the brown stains of rainwater and eroded soil extending from the mouths of rivers and wadis (ephemeral streams) far out into the sea. I recall, when on a field trip into the Negev Desert, I was shown the remarkable efforts made by Nabatean farmers two millennia ago in collecting the water from winter flash-floods, storing it in rock-cut cisterns and utilizing it very effectively in the spring and summer, in the terrace agriculture that they carried out in the dry riverbeds.

Large-scale water conservation schemes are long-term projects, and today politicians are reluctant to take on ventures that are likely to be completed after their terms of office have come to an end. One way around this quandary is to find a philanthropist, someone who can help cover the cost of major projects and is willing to do so for the benefit of the community as a whole. At a time of drought during the reign of King Amaury (1163–1174), a certain wealthy private citizen joined forces with the king in an effort to alleviate a serious shortage of drinking water experienced by the citizens of Jerusalem, and with the intention of improving the supply for future years. As in other cities in the Middle East, most of the drinking water came from rainwater collected in underground cisterns, and with a decrease in winter rains, these had emptied out. Additional sources of supply were urgently needed. A document dated a few years later (1176), but looking back on that period, records that Rainald, a minister of the Church of Mount Syon (Mount Zion) had given the king a vineyard at the foot of the mountain, below the house of a certain Germanus (elsewhere Germain), together with another small vineyard to the south, at the nearby crossroads (presumably the junction of the road that descends from David's Gate and continues up Mount Zion, with the road leading to Bethlehem).[6] These were exchanged for a vineyard next to the church of St. Procopius, which was located further to the south in the Valley of Hinnom. The document stated that the purpose of this exchange was to enable the construction of a pool "for the use of all Christians." This exchange seems to have been done with the aid of Germain and it was probably he who provided the financing for a huge dam that was constructed across the valley.[7] When the winter rains came, the area above (north of) the dam was flooded and formed what became known as the Pool of Germain (*lacus Germani/lac Germains*).

Jerusalem had several open reservoirs, both within and outside the city walls. Some of these were ancient, and this new one may have been a reconstitution of an earlier pool, possibly the Serpent's Pool mentioned by Josephus Flavius (*Bellum Judaicum*, bk. 5, chap. 3, §2) that contained water collected from the surrounding slopes and over-flow from the

---

6 *Regesta Regni Hierosolymitani, 1097–1291*, ed. Gustav Reinhold Röhricht (Innsbruck: Libraria academica Wagneriana, 1893), no. 536. Summary on *Revised Regesta Regni Hierosolymitani* internet, record no. 970: http://crusades-regesta.com/database?search_api_views_fulltext=Germanus&f%5B0%5D=field_grantor%3ARainaldus%20ecclesie%20Montis%20Syon%20minister, accessed June 16, 2022.

7 This dam can still be seen today, standing to its full height, and probably restored by the Ottoman Sultan Barkuk (1382–1389) together with the construction of a fountain (*sebil*). In 1536 the fountain was restored by Sultan Suleiman the Magnificent.

Herodian lower aqueduct from Bethlehem that ran adjacent to it. Today it is known as the Sultan's Pool due to its having been restored by the Mamluk sultan, Barkuk at the end of the fourteenth century, and rebuilt in the sixteenth century by the great Ottoman sultan, Suleiman the Magnificent. The transaction between Amaury and the abbey of Mount Syon appears to have taken place in the late 1160s, and in 1169 the reservoir was observed by Theoderich, who referred to it as the *nova cisterna*:

> Whosoever passes out of the western gate of the city near the Tower of David, and directs his path towards the south, will pass through the valley of Ennon, which skirts two sides of the city near the new cistern...[8]

Neither Theoderich, nor the document recording the transaction between the king and the abbey, mentions Germain as the instigator of this project, but this fact is recorded in the French text known as *The Condition of the City of Jerusalem*:

> Going down the hill (Mount Zion) you came to a pool in the valley called Germain's Pool, because a citizen of that name had it made to collect rainwater coming down from the hills; the city's horses were watered there.[9]

And, in support of his involvement in this project, there are also references to Germain having, at a later time, carried out additional public works intended to improve the water supply to the city. These later works date to 1185 when another drought struck the region, and not very long before the fall of Jerusalem to Saladin after the Battle of Hattin. The

---

8 *Theoderich's Description of the Holy Places*, trans. Stewart, 5, 51.

9 Janet Shirley, *Crusader Syria in the Thirteenth Century* (Aldershot: Ashgate, 1999), 19–20. Confusion has resulted by an erroneous earlier translation that referred to as the German Lake "because a certain German here collected the waters..."—*La Citez de Jherusalem: The City of Jerusalem Translated from the Old French*, trans. Charles R. Conder, Library of the Palestine Pilgrims' Text Society 6, no. 2 (London: Palestine Pilgrims' Text Society, 1888), 20.

drought of 1185–1186, coming shortly after an even more serious four-year drought of 1178–1181, threatened not only the citizens of Jerusalem, but the entire kingdom. It occurred in a particularly unstable period during the minority of King Baldwin V, and the situation was so desperate and food supplies so bad that the regent, Raymond of Tripoli, went so far as to make a treaty with Saladin, according to the terms of which the Ayyubids would supply the Franks with food. This is pretty remarkable if we consider the enduring enmity between the two sides, and the fact that the Frankish and Ayyubid armies would meet just two years hence on the battlefield at Hattin. According to a thirteenth century text, Germain:

> ...very eager to do good for the sake of God, had marble basins set up in the walls at three points in the city...and at each of these basins he had two cups attached by chains, and he always kept them full of water. Any man or woman could go there to drink.[10]

In an additional effort to improve the water supply at that time, he brought workmen to clear an ancient well (*Ain Rogel/ Bir Ayyub*) south of the city walls and set above it an antiliya wheel (a large, horse-turned wheel that lowered jars into the well and brought them up full of water). He even supplied his own horses to run the wheel night and day and paid to have men and packhorses carry the water from the well to the basins he had earlier set up in the city.

The most notable of Germain's efforts, however, was the aforementioned reservoir that once carried his name. Today, drained of its winter waters, it functions as an open-air concert venue.

It is rather sad to think that probably not one of the hundreds of people casually sipping water from a plastic bottle

---

10 *The Old French Continuation of William of Tyre 1184–1197*, in *The Conquest of Jerusalem and the Third Crusade: Sources in Translation*, ed. and trans. Peter Edbury, Crusade Texts in Translation 1 (Aldershot: Ashgate, 2007), 16.

Figure 12. Sultan's Pool (Germain's Pool), Jerusalem.

beneath the great stone wall that Germain long ago built across the valley, has the slightest idea who he was, or indeed that he ever existed. Times have changed, but the old problems remain, awaiting perhaps a new Germain to help resolve them.

Saladin

It is hardly surprising that we, the observers, the ordinary people, those of us who are not in the public eye, the "average Joes" to use the American terminology, tend to have little faith in the trustworthiness of our leaders and in the reliability of their decision-making. Politicians often seem to place their own needs above those of their voting public. Despite our repeated disappointment, they somehow periodically manage to raise our expectations with election promises, only to dash them a soon as they are securely in power. And against our better judgement we empower them time and again through the ballet box, foolishly hoping against hope that this time they will place our needs foremost. It is difficult to explain this behaviour, rather like that of an abused wife who return to her momentarily repentant husband. Few enough are the politicians who, having received our support, remain faithful to their pre-election declarations.

This is not to say that people who go into public life do not initially have good intentions. It is simply that along the way they discover that political life necessitates making concessions. And perhaps it is our appreciation of this that allows us to overlook their repeated transgressions. Politics is the art of compromise. But even the less cynical politicians, those that appear to be directed by ideology rather than self-interest, as they advance in public life often lose sight of the public that supported them. They seem, without even being aware of the fact, to put aside their good intentions and come to see their personal advance as the endgame. They are convinced, or convince themselves, that what appears to be in their best interest must also be in ours, and they increasingly come to believe what they say, rather than say what they believe. And who can blame them? Politicians who are not flexible, who refuse to go against their principles, are regarded as morally decent, but weak, not leadership material, lacking the necessary "killer instinct." And how sad it is that we should want our leaders to possess the brutality that appears to be a prerequisite to achieving and maintaining political power.

But perhaps I am being too harsh. To be fair, even some politicians whose moral compasses have become corrupt, occasionally revert to former good intentions, and are capable of recovering something of their fundamental decency. While this is far from typical, every so often one encounters a political leader who places the needs of his constituency before personal gain, who is willing to put everything on the line, even, in exceptional cases, his very life, in order to do the right thing. The former Egyptian president, Anwar Sadat, is I think, a prime example of this. Once he had established his leadership and popularity through what was regarded in Egypt as a great military victory in 1973, he took an astonishing risk, throwing caution to the winds, and did what he believed to be beneficial for his people. The result was a peace agreement that, for all its shortcomings, changed the face of the region to the great benefit of the people of both Egypt and Israel. He did so, undoubtedly with an awareness of the price he might have to pay and, as indeed, he subsequently did pay. Whatever criticisms might be raised today for his actions before and after his decision to make peace with his enemy, this was a rare example of exceptionally bold and moral behaviour by a political leader. I recall, at the time I was briefly living in Rome, the intensely emotional effect of his decision to go to Jerusalem. It was one of the most dramatic and moving episodes in the turbulent history of the Middle East, one that brought hope to the people of the region and for a time to the entire world.

One of the most admired leaders in the Middle Ages was Saladin. Like any political and religious leader of his time, his actions were occasionally cruel and certainly would warrant condemnation today, when far lesser sins are castigated, and words spoken long ago, are enough to put an end to long-esteemed legacies. We set ourselves high moral standards and believe that they are the ultimate truth with regard to how human beings should relate to one another, but we tend to spend too much energy these days condemning leaders of the past, holding up to inequitable scrutiny our past heroes. It is easy to understand why we should condemn a Stalin or a Pol Pot, but when, during a surge of moral righteousness sweeping across the Atlantic it becomes necessary to encase the statue of Winston Churchill at Westminster in a box in order to protect it from being vandalized by a new set of moral guard dogs, for whom, it seems, no historical character is beyond reach, one might ask, where will it all end? Churchill certainly had his share of flaws, and he was no doubt responsible for several injustices and calamities, not least in the debacle at Gallipoli. But we cannot dismiss his ultimate role in uniting the Western world against the tyranny of fascism. Those who so easily condemn display an arrogance that is not the prerogative of any fair observer of the past. If we are to go by these new moral standards, there can be no commemoration of past heroes. And how sad that would be! We would have to remove portraits from coins and postage stamps, rename airports, chip the heads off Mount Rushmore and shatter the statues of Roman emperors in European museums. And what would we gain? Certainly, we can do with less uncritical hero-worshiping, but we can still admire the achievements of great generals, patrons, founders of movements and of states, artists, philosophers, scientists, leaders in whatever field.

In Israel, few heroes are commemorated with statues. One of the better-known exceptions is a colourful statue of the founder of the Jewish state, David Ben Gurion located at the beach in Tel Aviv. It displays a caricatured version of the beloved elderly leader wearing only swimming trunks and standing on his head, old father William style. It is a demonstration of Israel's founder's proclivity to a somewhat eccentric form of physical exercise, but it makes this man, who might otherwise seem rather daunting, more human, accessible, endearing... and forgivable. Imagine what positive effect it might have on the people of Pyongyang if such a statue of the beloved founding father of North Korea were to be erected there.

In character with other leaders of his time, Saladin was on occasion brutal and merciless, but one cannot but find remarkable the humane gestures he at times displayed in his relationship towards the Christian enemy. Here are a few examples. In 1174, when he learnt of the death of King Amaury, Saladin sent a condolence letter to the king's brother, Baldwin IV.[11] It appears to be a very compassionate and sincere letter. He spoke of Amaury as "the just and greatest king" and he heaped praise and good wishes on the new king, referring to him as "glorified" and wishing him a long reign, fortune, felicity, wealth, and long-lasting success. True, in another letter that Saladin wrote to his nephew Farrukh-Shah, he referred to Amaury in a disparaging tone: "May God curse him and abandon him and lead him to punishment...."[12] You might as well ask, is this not the usual hypocrisy and cynicism that we are led to expect from politicians? Perhaps. The letter to Baldwin has been seen by some historians as diplomatic usage, but it might, after all, be both diplomatic and sincere.

---

11 Elon Harvey, "Saladin Consoles Baldwin IV over the Death of his Father," *Crusades* 15 (2017): 27–33.

12 Malcolm Cameron Lyons and D. E. P. Jackson, *Saladin: The Politics of Holy War* (Cambridge; Cambridge University Press, 1982), 75.

Leaders are sometimes required to use very different words when addressing different audiences, particularly in those cases where the two audiences are in a state of enmity. One gets a sense that, in writing to Baldwin, the sultan was indeed expressing genuine feelings, whereas to his nephew it was a case of political pragmatism, and he was stating what was expected and required of him. This appears to be supported by evidence of the reciprocal amicable relations that had developed between Amaury and Saladin following the former's siege of Alexandria in August 1167 and it is in line with other examples of Saladin's relationships with Christian leaders.[13] In 1183 Saladin besieged the desert castle of Karak. At the time, this remarkable fortress was in the possession of Saladin's most hated enemy, the obstreperous Raynald de Châtillon, a man who four years later Saladin would personally behead after defeating the Franks at the Battle of Hattin. However, on this occasion Saladin displayed an example of exceptional civility towards Raynald's stepson, Humphrey IV of Toron, who was in the castle celebrating his marriage to King Baldwin IV's younger half-sister, Isabella. In the version of these events recorded by the chronicler Ernoul, Raynald's wife and the groom's mother, Stephanie de Milly, requested that the besieging sultan avoid attacking the tower in which the newly married young couple were lodged. Although he continued to bombard the rest of the fortress, Saladin, with decided chivalry, indeed complied.[14] It is rather hard to imagine such consideration towards an enemy in today's conflicts.

Saladin behaved honourably with King Guy when he took him captive at Hattin in July 1187, in the famous episode that is recorded to have taken place in the sultan's tent, when he offered the king to drink from his goblet as a gesture of protection (a gesture that did not extend to Raynald when Godfrey passed the goblet on to him). Shortly afterwards, when he besieged Jerusalem in September–October, Saladin

---

13 Harvey, "Saladin Consoles Baldwin IV," 28–29.

14 Ernoul, *Chronique d'Ernoul et de Bernard le Trésorier*, ed. L. de Mas Latrie (Paris: Renouard, 1871), 103.

reached an equitable ransom agreement with the Frankish leaders. He allowed the citizens to keep many of their possessions, and he was not overly harsh in carrying out the ransom collection, even permitting many of the poor to depart without making the payment at all. He set up guards in all the streets of the city to protect the Christians from any harm before they departed, and then had them escorted in safety to Christian territory. He permitted the widows of his arch enemy Raynald and of King Amaury to leave the city without payment, and more remarkably still, he allowed the patriarch to carry away with him the valuable treasures of the Church of the Holy Sepulchre. He also refused to allow the destruction of the Church of the Holy Sepulchre. For all these acts Saladin faced harsh criticism from his own people. The sultan had very cordial relations with Richard I during the Third Crusade, and he showed great concern when the English king fell ill in 1192, agreeing to a truce, even though he could have taken advantage of Richard's indisposition. No leader lacks in failings and Saladin certainly had many in his various roles as administrator, military strategist, and tactician. But by the standards of the time in which he lived, certainly if we compare him to Baibars, the Mamluk leader who continued the holy war against the Crusader states in the following century, Saladin comes across as a man who on occasion was capable of remarkably moral and humane conduct. He is one of the few medieval leaders who gained the respect not only of his followers, but of his opponents as well.

Postscript

Hit and Myth—History and Mystery

This book has two underlying themes: the Crusader period, which is the bit of history and archaeology I have chosen to spend a career studying, and the notion of repetition in history. The first theme is fairly straightforward—the Crusader period is a phase of history, easily defined. The second is more complex, for it is a human perception, not so much a fact as a feeling, and consequently enigmatic, and perhaps dubious, but certainly fascinating.

Does history indeed repeat itself? Mark Twain is said to have suggested an alternative: "History doesn't repeat itself, but it often rhymes." Whether the attribution is correct (it has never been substantiated), this certainly Twain-like statement contains, as does any decent witticism, a subtle truth. For what is a rhyme? Not a repetition of the same word with the same meaning, but rather the following of one word by another that merely sounds the same. In a similar manner, what appears to be the repetition of a historical event is generally not that at all. Human history is old enough for there to be very little that is entirely new. If we take the earliest known use of stone tools by hominins at the end of the Pleistocene period, that is around 3.3 million years ago, to be the beginning of human history, we can appreciate that it would be remarkable indeed if a precursor could not be found for virtually any historical occurrence.

It seems that we are quick to grasp at the idea of repetition, perhaps because what is new is unknown, and what is unknown is frightening. When it landed upon us early in 2020, the COVID-19 pandemic was immediately compared to the fourteenth-century Black Plague, and the Spanish Flu of 1918-1920. The comparison was perhaps a mildly comforting one, for although those pandemics decimated populations in many parts of the world, humanity made it through. And there was reassurance in the fact that with modern medical knowledge and technology we are today so much better equipped to face such disasters. There is comfort in comparison. And so, we say, "history has repeated itself," and hold up examples like the attacks on Pearl Harbor and 9/11. And let's not get bogged down by the many details that challenge these comparisons. Indeed, it is not only the comfort they provide that appeals to us. If historical repetition is a reality, then, having been forewarned we have the opportunity to avoid repeating past mistakes—an opportunity that one ignores at one's own risk, as Hitler did when, on invading Russia in 1941, he did not take into consideration what "General Winter" had done to the French Grande Armée in 1812.

Other than seeking comfort and avoiding mistakes, perhaps it is simply easier for us to consider an event of the past if we compare it to something that we have personally experienced or are better acquainted with. Through my own recollections, together with things that I have heard or read about, I have tried to show that while the past may be over, it is often reflected in later events. And, if we think about it, such historical reverberations are not all that remarkable. If desperation combined with religious zeal caused the crusaders battling outside Antioch in 1098 to imagined that they saw mounted warriors ride down from the heaven to join them in the desperate battle, why should not the same thing happen a millennium later to equally fraught British soldiers on a field in Flanders? Perhaps the real lesson from this is that, however much things around us might change, we are fundamentally no different from our ancestors. Herein, hopefully, lies the value of this little book, in demonstrating that the past remains relevant, and that studying it is not an indulgence, but an act of genuine worth. History may not seem practical.

It is not a science. Nor, though its methodology sometimes makes it seem so, is archaeology. But it is useful, it is fascinating, and above all, it is mysterious. I suppose the latter quality is what most draws me to it. When the Oxford dean, Reverend William Spooner contorted his words and made the famous "spoonerism" that my father so liked to quote: "You have hissed all my mystery lectures. In fact, you have tasted two whole worms," his delightful miscoordination of the brain seems to have been expounding a profound truth.

Further Reading

General

Boas, Adrian J., ed. *The Crusader World*. London: Routledge, 2017.
    A broad-ranged collection of studies of the crusades and the Latin East by some of the most important scholars in the field.

Richard, Jean. *The Crusades, c. 1071–c. 1291*. Cambridge: Cambridge University Press, 1996.
    An excellent and erudite summary of the crusades and the Holy Land under Frankish rule by one of the great French historians of the crusader period.

Tyreman, Christopher. *God's War. A New History of the Crusades*. Cambridge, MA: Belknap, 2008.
    An up-to-date and well-written account of Crusading history and the Latin states.

Archaeology, Art, and Architecture

Boas, Adrian J. *Crusader Archaeology. The Material Culture of the Latin East*. London: Routledge, 1999; 2nd ed. 2017.
    A survey of material culture in its broadest sense in the crusader states.

—— . *Jerusalem in the Time of the Crusades*. London: Routledge, 2001.
    Examines all aspects of the Holy City, its population, buildings and institutions under Crusader rule.

Folda, Jaroslav. *The Art of the Crusaders in the Holy Land 1098–1187*. Cambridge: Cambridge University Press, 1995.

> A comprehensive and highly illustrated study of all aspects of artistic creation in the kingdom of Jerusalem prior to the Battle of Hattin, including architecture, sculpture, mosaics, frescos, manuscripts, icons, ivory carvings, metalwork, and coins.

——. *Crusader Art in the Holy Land, from the Third Crusade to the Fall of Acre: 1187–1291*. Cambridge: Cambridge University Press, 2005.

> Continues the examination of Frankish architecture and the figural art in the kingdom of Jerusalem after the fall of the Holy City in 1187 up to the fall of Acre in 1291.

Kennedy, Hugh. *Crusader Castles*. Cambridge: Cambridge University Press, 1995.

> A very useful compact discussion of Frankish military architecture.

Pringle, Denys. *The Churches of the Crusader Kingdom of Jerusalem*. 4 vols. Cambridge: Cambridge University Press, 1993–2009.

> The most extensive coverage of Frankish ecclesiastical architecture in the kingdom of Jerusalem.

Characters

Hamilton, Bernard. *The Leper King and his Heirs. Baldwin IV and the Crusader Kingdom of Jerusalem*. Cambridge: Cambridge University Press, 2000.

> An excellent study of one of the tragic figures of crusader history that challenges the traditional view of Baldwin IV's reign as a period of decline and failings.

Lyons, Malcolm Cameron, and D. E. P. Jackson. *Saladin. The Politics of the Holy War*. Cambridge: Cambridge University Press, 1997.

> A classic study of the Ayyubid sultan that makes use of previously unpublished Arabic sources to describe Saladin's career and achievements.

Phillips, Jonathan. *The Life and Legend of the Sultan Saladin*. London, Vintage, 2019.

> An excellent and highly readable recent study of the life and influence of Saladin.

Society

Hillenbrand, Carole. *The Crusades. Islamic Perspectives*. Edinburgh: Edinburgh University Press, 1999.

> Making extensive use of Muslim sources, this book examines the Muslim view of the crusades and Frankish society in the Latin East. It considers how the Muslims reacted to the Franks and what sort of influence their presence in the Levant had upon their neighbours.

Prawer, Joshua. *Crusader Institutions*. Oxford: Clarendon, 1980.

> A pioneering study of the institutions, economy, settlement, social, constitutional, military and legal history of the kingdom of Jerusalem

Pringle, Denys, ed. and trans. *Pilgrimage to Jerusalem and the Holy Land, 1187–1291*. Crusade Texts in Translation. Abingdon: Routledge, 2016.

> A useful study of the later pilgrim accounts of travel to and within the Latin East.

Warfare

Marshall, Christopher. *Warfare in the Latin East, 1192–1291*. Cambridge: Cambridge University Press, 1992.

> An excellent companion to R. C. Smail's classic *Crusading Warfare*, covering the period from the Third Crusade to the fall of the Crusader states in 1291.

Phillips, Jonathan. *The Second Crusade. Extending the Frontiers of Christendom*. New Haven: Yale University Press, 2007.

> Discusses the genesis, planning and execution of the botched Second Crusade.

Smail, R. C., *Crusading Warfare, 1097–1193*. Cambridge: Cambridge University Press, 1956.

>A classic work on all aspects of crusader warfare, examining the Christian and Muslim armies, military tactics and fortifications.

Tibble, Steve. *The Crusader Strategy. Defending the Holy Land*. New Haven: Yale University Press, 2020.

>An up-to-date study of the various means by which the Franks in the twelfth century faced the overwhelmingly greater enemy forces.

Printed and bound by CPI Group (UK) Ltd, Croydon, CR0 4YY

12/06/2024

14514476-0001